FAVORITE BRAND NAME™

LOW-FAT NO-FAT RECIPES

Publications International, Ltd.
Favorite Brand Name Recipes at www.fbnr.com

Pictured on the front cover: Chicken Roll-Up *(page 110).*

Pictured on the back cover *(top to bottom):* Grilled Vegetables *(page 172)* and Lemon Raspberry Tiramisu *(page 214).*

ISBN: 0-7853-9904-6

Library of Congress Control Number: 2004102736

Manufactured in China.

8 7 6 5 4 3 2 1

Nutritional Analysis: The nutritional information that appears with each recipe was submitted in part by the participating companies and associations. Every effort has been made to check the accuracy of these numbers. However, because numerous variables account for a wide range of values for certain foods, nutritive analyses in this book should be considered approximate.

Microwave Cooking: Microwave ovens vary in wattage. Use the cooking times as guidelines and check for doneness before adding more time.

Preparation/Cooking Times: Preparation times are based on the approximate amount of time required to assemble the recipe before cooking, baking, chilling or serving. These times include preparation steps such as measuring, chopping and mixing. The fact that some preparations and cooking can be done simultaneously is taken into account. Preparation of optional ingredients and serving suggestions is not included.

Contents

Low-Fat for Life!

It's simple: to lose weight, you have to use more calories than you consume. And since fat has nearly two times as many calories as either protein or carbohydrate, cutting fat is the quickest and easiest way to cut calories. Combine this with regular exercise, and you're on your way to weight loss success!

Plus, by limiting the fat you eat, you won't only be cutting calories. You'll be reducing your chances of heart disease, cancer and even diabetes. Saturated fats (found mainly in animal products and coconut oil, palm kernel oil and palm oil), hydrogenated fats (in processed foods such as crackers and cookies) and cholesterol are notorious for contributing to a person's chances of getting these health problems. If you eat less fat, you'll also be consuming less of these unhealthy types of fat.

Making a change to low-fat living is a lifestyle change. And despite common thought, it doesn't have to mean major sacrifices. You can still eat foods that taste good without spending a lot of time in the kitchen. The key word is "substitute." Find low-fat alternatives to the foods you love and new ways to prepare and season foods without fat. You'll be more apt to stick with your new low-fat way of life. This cookbook provides over 100 low-fat and no-fat recipes you're going to love.

The American Heart Association recommends healthy adults limit their fat intake to no more than 30% of daily calorie amounts. One gram of fat is equal to 9 calories. So, on a 1,500-calorie meal plan, a person would consume 50 grams or less of fat per day.

$$1{,}500 \text{ calories} \times (.30) = 450 \text{ calories}$$
$$450 \text{ calories} \div 9 \text{ calories} = 50 \text{ grams of fat per day}$$

Sometimes, counting fat grams is more trouble than it's worth. Your best bet is to simply try to eat fat-free and low-fat as often as possible.

Here are some tips to help you stay on track with your new low-fat lifestyle:

• Low-fat eating doesn't have to mean an end to good foods. Take advantage of the delicious recipes in low-fat cookbooks just like this one!

• Always have fresh fruits and vegetables on hand. Bring some to work with you, too. They are a great fat-free alternative to the high-fat, nutrient-deprived foods in vending machines.

• Get rid of high-fat foods and snacks in your house. You won't indulge if the temptation's not there. Instead, snack on fat-free high-fiber fruits, vegetables and whole-grain crackers.

• Eat more fiber-rich fruits, vegetables, legumes and whole grains. Fiber gives the feeling of fullness without all the extra fat calories.

• Drink plenty of water and other fluids throughout the day to keep the extra fiber moving through your system. Not only do these liquids aid in digestion, they also help you feel full. In fact, we often think we're hungry when our bodies actually just need a glass of water.

• Use fat-free and low-fat products in place of their high-fat counterparts. Fat-free and low-fat salad dressings, mayonnaise, sour cream, cheeses and yogurt are just a few examples of products on the market today. Most of them can be used without greatly affecting the flavors of the finished dishes. Or try mixing the fat-free version with the low-fat version.

• If you typically drink whole milk, try 2% for a while. You'll notice a difference at first. But it won't be long until you likely prefer the reduced-fat 2% version over the whole version. Next, try 1% milk, and finally fat-free (skim). Many people who swear they'll drink nothing other than whole milk, with time, often find they tend to prefer skim milk.

• Spread jams and jellies, rather than butter and margarine, on breads.

• Prepare more mixed meat and vegetable dishes. Cut the amount of meat in the recipe by one third and increase the amount of vegetables by one third.

Shop Smart

• Make a shopping list and stick to it. Eat a snack before shopping, and you'll be more likely to buy only the foods on your list. Choose a specific time to do your grocery shopping each week. Pick a time when the store won't be busy and you can move quickly through the aisles. You'll be less likely to make impulse purchases.

• Read the Nutrition Facts labels on foods. Choose brands with the least amount of fat and cholesterol. Here are the meanings behind some common terms you'll find on products:

> • Reduced-Fat or Less-Fat: At least 25% less fat than a standard serving of the regular food

> • Low-Fat: 3 grams of fat or less per serving

> • Fat-Free: Foods with 0.5 grams of fat or less per serving

• Buy fresh, in-season produce for the most flavor. The more flavor, the less fat you'll need to make a great-tasting dish.

• Experiment. Try grains, legumes, fruits and vegetables you've always wanted to try but never have.

Meat, Poultry and Fish

• Buy lean cuts of meat and trim off any visible fat before cooking. Remove the skin from poultry or buy skinless pieces from your grocer.

• Purchase extra-lean ground round, pork and turkey. Drain and rinse the liquid fat off the meat after it is cooked and before adding the other ingredients.

• Use extra-lean ground round for meat loaf, meatballs and other recipes for which it is difficult to drain excess fat.

• Choose boneless, skinless chicken breasts instead of drumsticks, thighs and wings.

• Buy "Select" beef cuts instead of "Choice" and "Prime" cuts with more marbling.

• "Loin" and "Round" signal leaner cuts of beef. "Loin" and "Leg" refer to leaner cuts of pork, lamb and veal.

• Use a fat separator or baster to remove the fat from soups, stews, sauces and casseroles. Or chill these dishes in the refrigerator overnight, then skim the congealed fat from the top of the food the next day.

• Make low-fat, high-fiber grain and vegetable dishes the main focus of your meals. Just use meat to add a bit of flavor.

• Roast lean meats and poultry on a rack to allow extra fat to drip off.

• Drain the fat from meats cooked in a skillet.

• Enjoy a meatless meal at least once a week. Refer to the Meatless chapter in this book for a delicious array of meatless dishes.

• Replace meat with fish a few times a week. Fish typically has less fat, and the fat it does have is the healthy unsaturated kind.

• Eat water-packed tuna instead of oil-packed tuna.

Food Preparation

• Bake, steam, roast, broil, grill, microwave, poach or boil instead of frying foods.

• Steam or grill vegetables.

• Buy the heaviest (best) nonstick skillets you can afford. You won't have to use any or as much fat for sautéing.

• Use flavored nonstick cooking sprays to keep foods from sticking to skillets and pans.

• Use only half the fat called for in your favorite recipes. If you are using the fat for sautéing, be sure to reduce the heat to medium-high and stir the food often.

• Measure any oil called for in a recipe. Don't just "eyeball" it.

• Buy a good wok. Stir-fry meats and vegetables in fat-free broth with very little change in taste or texture.

• Cook vegetables in flavored liquids such as wine, fat-free broth, bouillon, tomato juice or sherry instead of butter and oil. Use as little water possible to cook foods. Water dilutes flavors.

• Replace the oil in baked goods with applesauce, mashed banana, puréed fruit or plain nonfat yogurt. Use the trial and error method to come up with the correct proportions. Start by substituting half the fat with the fat-free replacement. Since low-fat foods tend to dry out easier than their full-fat counterparts, be sure to keep an eye on them during the last five minutes of baking. And try to keep the oven door closed until these last five minutes of baking, since foods made with fat-free replacements are particularly sensitive to changes in oven temperature.

• Substitute 2 egg whites or $1/4$ cup egg substitute for 1 egg.

• Add spice to your fat-free and low-fat meals. Spices compensate for the lack of fat, adding loads of incomparable flavor. Use spices, herbs, marinades, flavored vinegars, fat-free salad dressings, cocktail sauce, lemon juice and salsa to flavor foods, instead of high-fat sauces and salad dressings, sour cream, butter and oils. Bring out the flavor in dry spices by toasting them in a pan over medium heat before adding them to foods.

• Use cornstarch, flour, rice, mashed potatoes or other puréed vegetables in place of cream and butter to thicken sauces and soups.

• Use balsamic vinegar to add delicious fat-free flavor to vegetables and salads.

Away from Home

• Try to eat out less, and eat less fast food. Bring a healthy packed lunch to work. If you don't have time to prepare it in the morning, pack and refrigerate it the night before.

• Snack at home before going out to eat. You'll have more control when you're ordering.

• Ask your server how a food is prepared, and ask for low-fat menu suggestions.

• Opt for yeast-type breads and rolls, which tend to be lower in fat than muffins, corn bread and biscuits.

• Steer clear of marinated salads (e.g., bean salads).

• Ask for salad dressings and sauces to be served on the side. Dip your fork into the salad dressing before picking up a bite of salad.

chapter one
Breakfasts

Brunch Strata

2 cups cholesterol-free egg substitute
1 can (10¾ ounces) reduced-fat condensed cream of celery
   soup, undiluted
1 cup fat-free (skim) milk
1 can (4 ounces) sliced mushrooms, drained (optional)
¼ cup sliced green onions
1 teaspoon dry mustard
½ teaspoon salt (optional)
¼ teaspoon black pepper
6 slices reduced-fat white bread, cut into 1-inch cubes
4 links reduced-fat precooked breakfast sausage, thinly sliced

1. Preheat oven to 350°F. Spray 2-quart baking dish with nonstick cooking spray; set aside.

2. Combine egg substitute, soup, milk, mushrooms, if desired, green onions, mustard, salt, if desired, and pepper in medium bowl; mix well.

3. Combine bread cubes, sausage and egg mixture in prepared baking dish; toss to coat. Bake 35 to 40 minutes or until set. Garnish as desired. **Makes 6 servings**

Nutrients per Serving (1 cup Strata):
Calories 155	Protein 15g
Fat 2g	Carbohydrate 20g
Calories from Fat 12%	Fiber 3g
Saturated Fat 1g	Sodium 642mg
Cholesterol 8mg	

Dietary Exchanges: 1½ Starch, 1½ Lean Meat

Brunch Strata

Sunrise French Toast

    2 cups cholesterol-free egg substitute
    ½ cup evaporated skimmed milk
    1 teaspoon grated orange peel
    1 teaspoon vanilla
    ¼ teaspoon ground cinnamon
    1 loaf (1 pound) Italian bread, cut into ½-inch-thick slices
        (about 20 slices)
    1 jar (10 ounces) no-sugar-added orange marmalade
      Powdered sugar (optional)
      Maple-flavored syrup (optional)

1. Preheat oven to 400°F. Combine egg substitute, milk, orange peel, vanilla and cinnamon in medium bowl. Set aside.

2. Spread 1 bread slice with 1 tablespoon marmalade to within ½ inch of edge. Top with another bread slice. Repeat with remaining bread and marmalade.

3. Spray griddle or large skillet with nonstick cooking spray; heat over medium heat until hot. Dip sandwiches in egg substitute mixture. Do not soak. Cook sandwiches in batches 2 to 3 minutes on each side or until golden brown.

4. Transfer toasted sandwiches to 15×10-inch jelly-roll pan. Bake 10 to 12 minutes or until sides are sealed. Dust with powdered sugar and serve with syrup, if desired.   **Makes 10 servings**

Nutrients per Serving (1 French Toast sandwich [without powdered sugar and syrup]):

Calories 216	Protein 8g
Fat 2g	Carbohydrate 41g
Calories from Fat 7%	Fiber <1g
Saturated Fat <1g	Sodium 344mg
Cholesterol <1mg	

Dietary Exchanges: 2 Starch, 1 Fruit, ½ Lean Meat

Sunrise French Toast

Farmstand Frittata

Nonstick cooking spray
1 medium red bell pepper, seeded and cut into thin strips
½ cup chopped onion
1 cup broccoli florets, blanched and drained
1 cup cooked, quartered, unpeeled red potatoes
1 cup cholesterol-free egg substitute
6 egg whites
1 tablespoon chopped fresh parsley
½ teaspoon salt
¼ teaspoon black pepper
½ cup (2 ounces) shredded reduced-fat Cheddar cheese

1. Spray large nonstick ovenproof skillet with cooking spray; heat over medium heat until hot. Add bell pepper and onion; cook and stir 3 minutes or until crisp-tender.

2. Add broccoli and potatoes; cook and stir 1 to 2 minutes or until heated through.

3. Whisk together egg substitute, egg whites, parsley, salt and black pepper in medium bowl.

4. Spread vegetables in even layer in skillet. Pour egg white mixture over vegetables. Cover; cook over medium heat 10 to 12 minutes or until egg mixture is set.

5. Meanwhile, preheat broiler. Sprinkle cheese over frittata. Broil 4 inches from heat 1 minute or until cheese is bubbly and golden brown. Cut into 4 wedges. **Makes 4 servings**

Nutrients per Serving (1 Frittata wedge [¼ of total recipe]):

Calories 163	Protein 17g
Fat 2g	Carbohydrate 19g
Calories from Fat 12%	Fiber 2g
Saturated Fat 1g	Sodium 686mg
Cholesterol 8mg	

Dietary Exchanges: 1 Starch, 1 Vegetable, 1½ Lean Meat

Farmstand Frittata

Oat Cakes with Fresh Fruit Topping

    1 pint hulled strawberries, raspberries or blueberries, divided
  $\frac{1}{2}$ cup sugar, divided
    2 tablespoons cornstarch
  $\frac{1}{2}$ cup water
    1 teaspoon lemon juice
  $\frac{1}{2}$ cup uncooked quick oats
    1 cup whole wheat flour
 $2\frac{1}{2}$ teaspoons baking powder
 $1\frac{1}{4}$ cups fat-free (skim) milk
  $\frac{1}{2}$ cup plain nonfat yogurt

1. Place half of strawberries in medium bowl; mash with potato masher. Slice remaining strawberries; set aside. (If using raspberries or blueberries, do not slice.)

2. Combine $\frac{1}{3}$ cup sugar and cornstarch in small saucepan. Add water; stir until cornstarch is dissolved. Cook and stir over medium heat until mixture comes to a boil. Add lemon juice and mashed strawberries; return to a boil. Remove from heat; let stand 15 minutes. Stir in sliced strawberries. Set aside.

3. Toast oats in small heavy skillet over medium heat, stirring constantly, 3 minutes or until slightly browned. Remove to medium bowl; cool 10 minutes. Stir in flour, baking powder and remaining sugar. Combine milk and yogurt in small bowl; stir into flour mixture just until all ingredients are moistened. (Batter will be lumpy.)

4. Coat nonstick griddle or large heavy skillet with nonstick cooking spray. Heat over medium heat until water droplets sprinkled onto griddle bounce off surface. Drop batter by scant $\frac{1}{4}$-cupfuls onto griddle; spread to form 4-inch-round cakes. Cook 2 minutes or until bubbles appear on entire surface of batter. Turn cakes; cook 2 minutes longer or until browned. Serve warm with fruit topping.

Makes 6 servings

Nutrients per Serving (2 Oat Cakes with $\frac{1}{3}$ cup Fruit Topping):

Calories 209	Protein 7g
Fat 1g	Carbohydrate 45g
Calories from Fat 5%	Fiber 4g
Saturated Fat <1g	Sodium 0mg
Cholesterol 1mg	

Dietary Exchanges: $1\frac{1}{2}$ Starch, 1 Fruit, $\frac{1}{2}$ Milk

Oat Cakes with Fresh Fruit Topping

Wild Rice Blueberry Muffins

1½ cups all-purpose flour
½ cup sugar
2 teaspoons baking powder
1 teaspoon ground cinnamon
½ teaspoon salt
½ cup skim milk
4 egg whites
¼ cup applesauce
1 cup fresh blueberries
1 cup well cooked, chopped wild rice

Spray nonstick cooking spray in muffin cups or use paper liners. Preheat oven to 400°F. Combine flour, sugar, baking powder, cinnamon and salt in large bowl. Combine milk, egg whites and applesauce in separate bowl. Sprinkle 1 tablespoon dry ingredients over blueberries. Fold liquid ingredients into dry ingredients. Coat blueberries with flour mixture; fold, with wild rice, into batter. Batter will be stiff. Fill prepared muffin cups ⅔ full. Bake 15 to 20 minutes or until wooden toothpick inserted into centers comes out clean.

Makes 12 muffins

Favorite recipe from **Minnesota Cultivated Wild Rice Council**

Nutrients per Serving (1 Muffin):

Calories 120	Protein 4g
Fat <1g	Carbohydrate 26g
Calories from Fat 2%	Fiber 1g
Saturated Fat <1g	Sodium 169mg
Cholesterol <1mg	

Dietary Exchanges: 1 Starch, ½ Fruit

Raisin-Streusel Coffee Cake

1½ cups all-purpose flour
  2 teaspoons baking powder
¼ teaspoon baking soda
¼ teaspoon salt
¾ cup granulated sugar
  2 tablespoons margarine, softened
¾ cup nonfat sour cream
  1 egg
  1 teaspoon vanilla extract
½ cup MOTT'S® Chunky Apple Sauce
⅓ cup firmly packed light brown sugar
¼ cup raisins
  2 tablespoons crunchy nut-like cereal nuggets

1. Preheat oven to 350°F. Spray 9-inch round cake pan with nonstick cooking spray.

2. In small bowl, combine flour, baking powder, baking soda and salt.

3. In large bowl, beat granulated sugar and margarine with electric mixer at medium speed until blended. Whisk in sour cream, egg and vanilla. Gently mix in apple sauce.

4. Add flour mixture to apple sauce mixture; stir until well blended. Pour batter into prepared pan.

5. In small bowl, combine brown sugar, raisins and cereal. Sprinkle over batter.

6. Bake 50 minutes or until toothpick inserted into center comes out clean. Cool 15 minutes on wire rack. Serve warm or cool completely. Cut into 14 wedges.   **Makes 14 servings**

Nutrients per Serving (1 wedge Coffee Cake):

Calories 160	Protein 3g
Fat 2g	Carbohydrate 32g
Calories from Fat 12%	Fiber 1g
Saturated Fat <1g	Sodium 175mg
Cholesterol 15mg	

Dietary Exchanges: 1 Starch, 1 Fruit, ½ Fat

Vegetable Medley Quiche

Nonstick cooking spray
2 cups frozen diced potatoes with onions and peppers, thawed
1 package (16 ounces) frozen mixed vegetables (such as
    zucchini, carrots and beans), thawed and drained
1 can (10¾ ounces) reduced-fat condensed cream of
    mushroom soup, undiluted, divided
1 cup cholesterol-free egg substitute
½ cup grated Parmesan cheese, divided
¼ cup fat-free (skim) milk
¼ teaspoon dried dill weed
¼ teaspoon dried thyme leaves
¼ teaspoon dried oregano leaves
    Dash salt and black pepper (optional)

1. Preheat oven to 400°F. Spray 9-inch pie plate with cooking spray; press potatoes onto bottom and side of pan to form crust. Spray potatoes lightly with cooking spray. Bake 15 minutes.

2. *Reduce oven temperature to 375°F.* Combine mixed vegetables, half of soup, egg substitute and ¼ cup cheese in small bowl; mix well. Pour egg mixture into potato shell; sprinkle with remaining ¼ cup cheese. Bake 35 to 40 minutes or until set.

3. Combine remaining soup, milk and seasonings in small saucepan; mix well. Simmer over low heat 5 minutes or until heated through. Serve sauce with quiche.   **Makes 6 servings**

Nutrients per Serving: (⅙ of total recipe [without salt and black pepper
                    seasonings])

Calories 129	Protein 9g
Fat 2g	Carbohydrate 19g
Calories from Fat 15%	Fiber 4g
Saturated Fat 2g	Sodium 436mg
Cholesterol 5mg	

Dietary Exchanges: 1 Starch, 1 Vegetable, ½ Lean Meat

Vegetable Medley Quiche

Cranberry-Orange Ring

2 cups all-purpose flour
1 cup sugar
1½ teaspoons baking powder
1 teaspoon salt
½ teaspoon baking soda
¼ teaspoon ground cloves
1 tablespoon minced orange peel
¾ cup orange juice
1 egg, lightly beaten
2 tablespoons vegetable oil
1 teaspoon vanilla
¼ teaspoon orange extract
1 cup whole fresh or frozen cranberries, thawed

1. Preheat oven to 350°F. Grease 12-cup tube pan; set aside.

2. Combine flour, sugar, baking powder, salt, baking soda and cloves in large bowl. Add orange peel; mix well. Set aside. Combine orange juice, egg, oil, vanilla and orange extract in medium bowl. Beat until well blended. Add orange juice mixture to flour mixture. Stir until just moistened. Gently fold in cranberries. Do not overmix.

3. Spread batter evenly into prepared pan. Bake 30 to 35 minutes or until toothpick inserted near center comes out clean. Cool in pan on wire rack 15 to 20 minutes. Invert onto serving plate. Cut into 12 slices. Serve warm or at room temperature. **Makes 12 servings**

Nutrients per Serving (1 cake slice [¹⁄₁₂ of total recipe]):

Calories 181	Protein 3g
Fat 3g	Carbohydrate 36g
Calories from Fat 15%	Fiber 1g
Saturated Fat <1g	Sodium 314mg
Cholesterol 18mg	

Dietary Exchanges: 2 Starch, ½ Fruit

Cranberry-Orange Ring

Triple Berry Breakfast Parfait

2 cups vanilla sugar-free nonfat yogurt
¼ teaspoon ground cinnamon
1 cup sliced strawberries
½ cup blueberries
½ cup raspberries
1 cup low-fat granola without raisins
    Mint leaves, for garnish (optional)

1. Combine yogurt and cinnamon in small bowl. Combine strawberries, blueberries and raspberries in medium bowl.

2. For each parfait, layer ¼ cup fruit mixture, 2 tablespoons granola and ¼ cup yogurt mixture in parfait glass. Repeat layers. Garnish with mint leaves, if desired. **Makes 4 servings**

Nutrients per Serving (½ Parfait):

Calories 236	Protein 9g
Fat 2g	Carbohydrate 49g
Calories from Fat 9%	Fiber 2g
Saturated Fat <1g	Sodium 101mg
Cholesterol 0mg	

Dietary Exchanges: 2 Starch, 1 Fruit, ½ Milk

Triple Berry Breakfast Parfaits

chapter two
Starters

Veggie Quesadilla Appetizers

   10 (8-inch) flour tortillas
   1 cup *each* finely chopped broccoli and thinly sliced mushrooms
   ¾ cup shredded carrots
   ¼ cup chopped green onions
   1¼ cups (5 ounces) shredded reduced-fat sharp Cheddar cheese
   2 cups Zesty Pico de Gallo (recipe follows)

Brush both sides of tortillas lightly with water. Heat small nonstick skillet over medium heat until hot. Heat tortillas, one at a time, 30 seconds on each side. Divide vegetables among 5 tortillas; sprinkle evenly with cheese. Top with remaining 5 tortillas. Cook quesadillas, one at a time, in large nonstick skillet or on griddle over medium heat 2 minutes on each side or until surface is crisp and cheese is melted. Cut each quesadilla into 4 wedges. Serve with Zesty Pico de Gallo. Garnish as desired.   **Makes 20 servings**

Zesty Pico de Gallo

   2 cups chopped seeded tomatoes
   1 cup chopped green onions
   1 can (8 ounces) tomato sauce
   ½ cup minced fresh cilantro
   1 to 2 tablespoons minced jalapeño peppers*
   1 tablespoon fresh lime juice

*Jalapeño peppers can sting and irritate the skin. Wear gloves when handling peppers and do not touch eyes. Wash hands after handling.

Combine all ingredients in medium bowl. Cover; refrigerate at least 1 hour.   **Makes 20 servings**

continued on page 28

Veggie Quesadilla Appetizer

Veggie Quesadilla Appetizers, continued

Nutrients per Serving (1 Quesadilla wedge with about 1½ tablespoons Zesty Pico de Gallo):

Calories 79	Protein 4g
Fat 2g	Carbohydrate 12g
Calories from Fat 21%	Fiber 1g
Saturated Fat 1g	Sodium 223mg
Cholesterol 4mg	

Dietary Exchanges: 1 Starch

Bruschetta

Nonstick cooking spray
1 cup thinly sliced onion
½ cup chopped seeded tomato
2 tablespoons capers
¼ teaspoon black pepper
3 cloves garlic, finely chopped
1 teaspoon olive oil
4 slices French bread
½ cup (2 ounces) shredded reduced-fat Monterey Jack cheese

1. Spray large nonstick skillet with nonstick cooking spray. Heat over medium heat until hot. Add onion. Cook and stir 5 minutes. Stir in tomato, capers and pepper. Cook 3 minutes.

2. Preheat broiler. Combine garlic and oil in small bowl; brush one side of each bread slice with mixture. Top with onion mixture and cheese. Place on baking sheet. Broil 3 minutes or until cheese melts.

Makes 4 servings

Nutrients per Serving (1 Bruschetta slice):

Calories 90	Protein 3g
Fat 2g	Carbohydrate 17g
Calories from Fat 20%	Fiber <1g
Saturated Fat <1g	Sodium 194mg
Cholesterol 0mg	

Dietary Exchanges: 1 Starch

Bruschetta

Spicy Orange Chicken Kabob Appetizers

2 boneless skinless chicken breasts (about 8 ounces)
1 small red or green bell pepper
24 small fresh button mushrooms
½ cup orange juice
2 tablespoons reduced-sodium soy sauce
1 tablespoon vegetable oil
1½ teaspoons onion powder
½ teaspoon Chinese five-spice powder

1. Cut chicken and pepper each into 24 (¾-inch) square pieces. Place chicken, pepper and mushrooms in large resealable plastic food storage bag. Combine orange juice, soy sauce, oil, onion powder and five-spice powder in small bowl. Pour over chicken mixture. Close bag securely; turn to coat. Marinate in refrigerator 4 to 24 hours, turning frequently.

2. Soak 24 small wooden skewers or toothpicks in water 20 minutes. Meanwhile, preheat broiler. Coat broiler pan with nonstick cooking spray.

3. Drain chicken, pepper and mushrooms, reserving marinade. Thread 1 piece chicken, 1 piece pepper and 1 mushroom onto each skewer. Place on prepared pan. Brush with marinade; discard any remaining marinade. Broil 4 inches from heat source 5 to 6 minutes or until chicken is no longer pink in center. Serve immediately.

Makes 12 servings

Nutrients per Serving (2 Kabobs):

Calories 30
Fat <1g
Calories from Fat 26%
Saturated Fat <1g
Cholesterol 10mg

Protein 4g
Carbohydrate 2g
Fiber <1g
Sodium 38mg

Dietary Exchanges: ½ Lean Meat

Spicy Orange Chicken Kabob Appetizers

Shrimp Toast

    12 large shrimp, shelled and deveined, with tails intact
     1 egg
    2½ tablespoons cornstarch
     ¼ teaspoon salt
      Dash black pepper
     3 slices white sandwich bread, crusts removed, quartered
     1 hard-cooked egg yolk, cut into ½-inch pieces
     1 slice (1 ounce) cooked ham, cut into ½-inch pieces
     1 green onion with top, finely chopped
      Vegetable oil for frying
      Green Onion Curls (recipe follows) and hard-cooked egg
        half, for garnish (optional)

1. Cut deep slit down back of each shrimp; press gently with fingers to flatten.

2. Beat 1 egg, cornstarch, salt and pepper in large bowl until blended. Add shrimp; toss to coat well.

3. Place 1 shrimp, cut side down, on each bread piece; press shrimp gently into bread.

4. Brush or rub small amount of leftover egg mixture onto each shrimp.

5. Place 1 piece each of egg yolk and ham and a scant ¼ teaspoonful onion on top of each shrimp.

6. Heat oil in wok or large skillet over medium-high heat to 375°F. Add 3 or 4 bread pieces at a time; cook until golden, 1 to 2 minutes on each side. Drain on paper towels. Garnish with Green Onion Curls, if desired.   **Makes 12 servings**

Green Onion Curls

    6 to 8 medium green onions with tops
      Cold water
  10 to 12 ice cubes

1. Trim bulbs (white part) from onions; reserve for another use, if desired. Cut remaining stems (green part) to 4-inch lengths.

continued on page 34

Shrimp Toast

Shrimp Toast, continued

2. Using sharp scissors, cut each section of green stems lengthwise into 6 to 8 very thin strips down to beginning of stems.

3. Fill large bowl about half full with cold water. Add green onions and ice cubes. Refrigerate until onions curl, about 1 hour; drain.

Makes 6 to 8 curls

Nutrients per Serving (1 Shrimp Toast [without garnish]):

Calories 45

Fat 1g

Calories from Fat 20%

Saturated Fat <1g

Cholesterol 47mg

Protein 3g

Carbohydrate 5g

Fiber <1g

Sodium 128mg

Dietary Exchanges: ½ Starch

Snappy Salsa Dip

1 package (8 ounces) fat-free cream cheese, softened
½ cup chunky salsa
1 tablespoon lime juice

1. Beat cream cheese in small bowl with electric mixer on medium speed until smooth. Add salsa and lime juice; mix until blended. Refrigerate until ready to serve.

2. Serve with tortilla chips or assorted fresh vegetables.

Makes 12 servings (1½ cups)

Prep Time: 5 minutes plus refrigerating

Nutrients per Serving (2 tablespoons Dip [without chips and vegetables]):

Calories 24

Fat <1g

Calories from Fat 10%

Saturated Fat <1g

Cholesterol 2mg

Protein 3g

Carbohydrate 2g

Fiber <1g

Sodium 180mg

Dietary Exchanges: ½ Lean Meat

Quick and Easy Stuffed Mushrooms

1 slice whole wheat bread
16 large mushrooms
$\frac{1}{2}$ cup sliced celery
$\frac{1}{2}$ cup sliced onion
1 clove garlic
  Nonstick cooking spray
1 teaspoon Worcestershire sauce
$\frac{1}{2}$ teaspoon dried marjoram leaves, crushed
$\frac{1}{8}$ teaspoon ground red pepper
  Dash paprika

1. Preheat oven to 350°F. Tear bread into pieces; place in food processor. Process 30 seconds or until crumbs form. Transfer to small bowl; set aside.

2. Remove stems from mushrooms; reserve caps. Place mushroom stems, celery, onion and garlic in food processor. Process with on/off pulses until vegetables are finely chopped.

3. Coat nonstick skillet with cooking spray. Add mushroom mixture; cook and stir over medium heat 5 minutes or until onion is tender. Remove to bowl. Stir in bread crumbs, Worcestershire sauce, marjoram and ground red pepper.

4. Fill mushroom caps with mixture, pressing down firmly. Place filled caps about $\frac{1}{2}$ inch apart in shallow baking pan. Spray tops lightly with cooking spray. Sprinkle with paprika. Bake 15 minutes or until hot.   **Makes 8 servings**

Note: Mushrooms may be stuffed up to 1 day ahead. Refrigerate filled mushroom caps, covered, until ready to serve. Bake in preheated 300°F oven 20 minutes or until hot.

Nutrients per Serving (2 Stuffed Mushroom caps):

Calories 20	Protein 1g
Fat <1g	Carbohydrate 4g
Calories from Fat 11%	Fiber 1g
Saturated Fat <1g	Sodium 29mg
Cholesterol 0mg	

Dietary Exchanges: 1 Vegetable

Roasted Garlic Spread with Three Cheeses

2 medium heads garlic
2 packages (8 ounces each) fat-free cream cheese, softened
1 package (3½ ounces) goat cheese
2 tablespoons (1 ounce) crumbled blue cheese
1 teaspoon dried thyme leaves
   Yellow bell pepper wedges, cucumber slices, carrots,
      radishes or crackers (optional)

1. Preheat oven to 400°F. Cut tops off garlic heads to expose tops of cloves. Place garlic in small baking pan; bake 45 minutes or until garlic is very tender. Remove from pan; cool completely. Squeeze garlic into small bowl; mash with fork.

2. Beat cream cheese and goat cheese with electric mixer at medium speed in small bowl until smooth; stir in blue cheese, garlic and thyme. Cover; refrigerate 3 hours or overnight.

3. Spoon dip into serving bowl; serve with yellow bell pepper wedges, cucumber slices, carrots, radishes or crackers, if desired. Garnish with fresh thyme and red bell pepper strip, if desired.

Makes 21 servings

Nutrients per Serving (2 tablespoons Spread [without dippers and garnish]):

Calories 37
Fat 1g
Calories from Fat 29%
Saturated Fat <1g
Cholesterol 9mg
Protein 4g
Carbohydrate 2g
Fiber <1g
Sodium 157mg

Dietary Exchanges: ½ Lean Meat

Roasted Garlic Spread with Three Cheeses

Vegetable & Couscous Filled Tomatoes

½ cup reduced-sodium chicken broth
2 teaspoons olive oil
⅓ cup uncooked quick-cooking couscous
18 large plum tomatoes
   Nonstick cooking spray
1 cup diced zucchini
⅓ cup sliced green onions
2 cloves garlic, minced
2 tablespoons finely chopped fresh Italian parsley
1½ teaspoons Dijon mustard
½ teaspoon dried Italian seasoning

1. Place chicken broth and oil in small saucepan; bring to a boil over high heat. Stir in couscous; cover. Remove saucepan from heat; let stand 5 minutes.

2. Cut thin slice from top of each tomato. Remove pulp, leaving ⅛-inch-thick shell; reserve pulp. Place tomatoes, cut side down, on paper towels to drain. Meanwhile, drain excess liquid from reserved pulp; chop pulp to measure ⅔ cup.

3. Spray large nonstick skillet with cooking spray; heat over medium heat until hot. Add zucchini, onions and garlic. Cook and stir 5 minutes or until vegetables are tender.

4. Combine couscous, reserved tomato pulp, vegetables, parsley, mustard and Italian seasoning in large bowl. Fill tomato shells evenly with couscous mixture. Garnish as desired.   **Makes 18 appetizers**

Nutrients per Serving (1 Filled Tomato [without garnish]):

Calories 65	Protein 2g
Fat 1g	Carbohydrate 13g
Calories from Fat 14%	Fiber 3g
Saturated Fat <1g	Sodium 20mg
Cholesterol 0mg	

Dietary Exchanges: ½ Starch, 1½ Vegetable

Vegetable & Couscous Filled Tomatoes

Pinwheel Appetizers

3 cups cooked wild rice
1 package (8 ounces) nonfat pasteurized process cream cheese product
$\frac{1}{3}$ cup grated Parmesan cheese
1 teaspoon dried parsley flakes
$\frac{1}{2}$ teaspoon garlic powder
$\frac{1}{2}$ teaspoon Dijon-style mustard
2 to 3 drops hot pepper sauce (optional)
3 (12-inch) soft flour tortillas
$2\frac{1}{2}$ ounces thinly sliced corned beef
9 fresh spinach leaves

Combine wild rice, cream cheese, Parmesan cheese, parsley, garlic powder, mustard and pepper sauce. Spread evenly over tortillas, leaving $\frac{1}{2}$-inch border on one side of each tortilla. Place single layer corned beef over rice and cheese mixture. Top with layer of spinach. Roll each tortilla tightly toward $\frac{1}{2}$-inch border. Moisten border of tortilla with water; press to seal roll. Wrap tightly in plastic wrap. Refrigerate several hours or overnight. Cut into 1-inch slices.

Makes 36 appetizers

Favorite recipe from **Minnesota Cultivated Wild Rice Council**

Nutrients per Serving (1 Pinwheel Appetizer):

Calories 37	Protein 2g
Fat 1g	Carbohydrate 5g
Calories from Fat 21%	Fiber <1g
Saturated Fat <1g	Sodium 91mg
Cholesterol 4mg	

Dietary Exchanges: $\frac{1}{2}$ Starch

Pinwheel Appetizers

Apricot-Chicken Pot Stickers

2 cups plus 1 tablespoon water, divided
2 boneless skinless chicken breasts (about 8 ounces)
2 cups chopped finely shredded cabbage
½ cup all-fruit apricot preserves
2 green onions with tops, finely chopped
2 teaspoons reduced-sodium soy sauce
½ teaspoon grated fresh ginger
⅛ teaspoon black pepper
30 (3-inch) wonton wrappers
   Prepared sweet-and-sour sauce (optional)

1. Bring 2 cups water to a boil in medium saucepan. Add chicken. Reduce heat to low; simmer, covered, 10 minutes or until chicken is no longer pink in center. Remove from saucepan; drain.

2. Add cabbage and remaining 1 tablespoon water to saucepan. Cook over high heat 1 to 2 minutes or until water evaporates, stirring occasionally. Remove from heat; cool slightly.

3. Finely chop chicken. Add to saucepan along with preserves, green onions, soy sauce, ginger and pepper; mix well.

4. To assemble pot stickers, remove 3 wonton wrappers at a time from package. Spoon slightly rounded tablespoonful chicken mixture onto center of each wrapper; brush edges of wrapper with water. Bring 4 corners together; press to seal. Repeat with remaining wrappers and filling.

5. Spray steamer with nonstick cooking spray. Assemble steamer so that water is ½ inch below steamer basket. Fill steamer basket with pot stickers, leaving enough space between them to prevent sticking. Cover; steam 5 minutes. Transfer pot stickers to serving plate. Serve with prepared sweet-and-sour sauce, if desired.

Makes 10 servings

Nutrients per Serving (3 Pot Stickers [without sweet-and-sour sauce]):

Calories 145	Protein 8g
Fat 1g	Carbohydrate 26g
Calories from Fat 6%	Fiber 1g
Saturated Fat <1g	Sodium 223mg
Cholesterol 17mg	

Dietary Exchanges: 1½ Starch, ½ Lean Meat

Apricot-Chicken Pot Stickers

Baked Spinach Balls

2 cups sage and onion or herb-seasoned bread stuffing mix
2 tablespoons grated Parmesan cheese
1 small onion, chopped
1 clove garlic, minced
1/4 teaspoon dried thyme leaves
1/4 teaspoon black pepper
1 package (10 ounces) frozen chopped spinach, thawed and well drained
1/4 cup fat-free reduced-sodium chicken broth
2 egg whites, beaten
Dijon or honey mustard (optional)

1. Combine bread stuffing mix, cheese, onion, garlic, thyme and pepper in medium bowl; mix well. Combine spinach, broth and egg whites in separate medium bowl; mix well. Stir into bread stuffing mixture. Cover; refrigerate 1 hour or until mixture is firm.

2. Preheat oven to 350°F. Shape mixture into 24 balls. Place on ungreased baking sheet; bake 15 minutes or until browned. Serve with mustard for dipping, if desired.   **Makes 12 servings**

Nutrients per Serving (2 Spinach Balls [without mustard]):

Calories 52	Protein 3g
Fat 1g	Carbohydrate 9g
Calories from Fat 12%	Fiber <1g
Saturated Fat <1g	Sodium 227mg
Cholesterol 1mg	

Dietary Exchanges: 1/2 Starch, 1/2 Vegetable

Crab Canapés

⅔ cup fat-free cream cheese, softened
2 teaspoons lemon juice
1 teaspoon hot pepper sauce
1 package (8 ounces) imitation crabmeat or lobster, flaked
⅓ cup chopped red bell pepper
2 green onions with tops, sliced (about ¼ cup)
64 cucumber slices (about 2½ medium cucumbers cut into
⅜-inch-thick slices) or melba toast rounds
Fresh parsley, for garnish (optional)

1. Combine cream cheese, lemon juice and hot pepper sauce in medium bowl; mix well. Stir in crabmeat, bell pepper and green onions; cover. Chill 1 hour or until ready to serve.

2. To serve, spoon 1½ teaspoons crabmeat mixture onto each cucumber slice. Place on serving plate; garnish with parsley, if desired. **Makes 16 servings**

Note: Chilling the crabmeat mixture allows the flavors to blend.

Nutrients per Serving: (4 Canapés made with cucumber slices):

Calories 31	Protein 4g
Fat <1g	Carbohydrate 4g
Calories from Fat 8%	Fiber <1g
Saturated Fat <1g	Sodium 178mg
Cholesterol 5mg	

Dietary Exchanges: ½ Lean Meat, ½ Vegetable

chapter three
Soups

Garden Gazpacho

    6 large ripe tomatoes, peeled and seeded
    $\frac{1}{2}$ cup coarsely chopped onion
    $\frac{1}{2}$ cup chopped seeded peeled cucumber
    $\frac{1}{2}$ cup coarsely chopped green bell pepper
    1 clove garlic, minced
    1 cup low-sodium tomato juice
    1 teaspoon lemon juice
    $\frac{1}{8}$ teaspoon black pepper
    $\frac{1}{8}$ teaspoon hot pepper sauce
       Plain nonfat yogurt (optional)

1. Combine tomatoes, onion, cucumber, bell pepper and garlic in food processor or blender. Process using on/off pulsing action just until mixture is thick and chunky. Transfer to medium bowl.

2. Stir in tomato juice, lemon juice, black pepper and hot pepper sauce. Cover and chill until ready to serve. Top with nonfat yogurt, if desired. Garnish as desired. **Makes 4 servings**

Nutrients per Serving ($1\frac{1}{4}$ cups Gazpacho [without yogurt topping and garnish]):

Calories 68	Protein 3g
Fat 1g	Carbohydrate 15g
Calories from Fat 9%	Fiber 4g
Saturated Fat <1g	Sodium 25mg
Cholesterol 0mg	

Dietary Exchanges: 3 Vegetable

Garden Gazpacho

Vegetable-Chicken Noodle Soup

1 cup chopped celery
1/2 cup thinly sliced leek (white part only)
1/2 cup chopped carrot
1/2 cup chopped turnip
6 cups fat-free reduced-sodium chicken broth, divided
1 tablespoon minced fresh parsley
1 1/2 teaspoons fresh thyme *or* 1/2 teaspoon dried thyme leaves
1 teaspoon fresh rosemary *or* 1/4 teaspoon dried rosemary
leaves
1 teaspoon balsamic vinegar
1/4 teaspoon black pepper
2 ounces uncooked yolk-free wide noodles
1 cup diced cooked chicken breast

1. Place celery, leek, carrot, turnip and 1/3 cup chicken broth in large saucepan. Cover; cook over medium heat until vegetables are tender, stirring occasionally.

2. Stir in remaining 5 2/3 cups chicken broth, parsley, thyme, rosemary, vinegar and pepper. Bring to a boil. Add noodles; cook until noodles are tender. Stir in chicken. Reduce heat to medium. Simmer until heated through. **Makes 6 servings**

Nutrients per Serving (1 bowl Soup [1/6 of total recipe]):

Calories 98	Protein 10g
Fat 2g	Carbohydrate 12g
Calories from Fat 14%	Fiber 1g
Saturated Fat <1g	Sodium 73mg
Cholesterol 18mg	

Dietary Exchanges: 1/2 Starch, 1/2 Vegetable, 1 Lean Meat

Vegetable-Chicken Noodle Soup

Black and White Chili

Nonstick cooking spray
1 pound chicken tenders, cut into ¾-inch pieces
1 cup coarsely chopped onion
1 can (15½ ounces) Great Northern beans, rinsed and drained
1 can (15 ounces) black beans, rinsed and drained
1 can (14½ ounces) Mexican-style stewed tomatoes, undrained
2 tablespoons Texas-style chili powder seasoning mix

1. Spray large saucepan with cooking spray; heat over medium heat until hot. Add chicken and onion; cook and stir over medium to medium-high heat 5 to 8 minutes or until chicken is browned.

2. Stir remaining ingredients into saucepan; bring to a boil. Reduce heat to low; simmer, uncovered, 10 minutes. Garnish as desired.

Makes 6 servings

Serving Suggestion: For a change of pace, this delicious chili is excellent served over cooked rice or pasta.

Prep and Cook Time: 30 minutes

Nutrients per Serving (1 cup Chili [without garnish]):

Calories 260	Protein 27g
Fat 2g	Carbohydrate 34g
Calories from Fat 6%	Fiber 8g
Saturated Fat <1g	Sodium 403mg
Cholesterol 44mg	

Dietary Exchanges: 2 Starch, 2 Lean Meat

Black and White Chili

Cioppino

 1 teaspoon olive oil
 1 large onion, chopped
 1 cup sliced celery, with celery tops
 1 clove garlic, minced
 4 cups water
 1 fish-flavor bouillon cube
 1 tablespoon salt-free Italian herb seasoning
 ¼ pound cod or other boneless mild-flavored fish fillets
 1 large tomato, chopped
 1 can (10 ounces) baby clams, rinsed and drained (optional)
 ¼ pound raw small shrimp, peeled and deveined
 ¼ pound raw bay scallops
 ¼ cup flaked crabmeat or crabmeat blend
 2 tablespoons fresh lemon juice

1. Heat olive oil in large saucepan over medium heat until hot. Add onion, celery and garlic. Cook and stir 5 minutes or until onion is soft. Add water, bouillon cube and Italian seasoning. Cover and bring to a boil over high heat.

2. Cut cod fillets into ½-inch pieces. Add cod and tomato to saucepan. Reduce heat to medium-low. Add clams, if desired, shrimp, scallops, crabmeat and lemon juice. Simmer 10 to 15 minutes or until seafood is opaque. **Makes 4 servings**

Prep and Cook Time: 30 minutes

Nutrients per Serving (1¾ cups Cioppino):

Calories 122	Protein 18g
Fat 2g	Carbohydrate 8g
Calories from Fat 18%	Fiber 2g
Saturated Fat <1g	Sodium 412mg
Cholesterol 75mg	

Dietary Exchanges: 1 Vegetable, 2 Lean Meat

Cioppino

Butternut Bisque

1 teaspoon margarine or butter
1 large onion, coarsely chopped
1 medium butternut squash (about 1½ pounds), peeled,
    seeded and cut into ½-inch pieces
2 cans (14½ ounces each) fat-free reduced-sodium chicken
    broth, divided
½ teaspoon ground nutmeg or freshly grated nutmeg
⅛ teaspoon white pepper
    Plain nonfat yogurt and chives, for garnish (optional)

1. Melt margarine in large saucepan over medium heat. Add onion;
cook and stir 3 minutes.

2. Add squash and 1 can chicken broth; bring to a boil over high
heat. Reduce heat to low; cover and simmer 20 minutes or until
squash is very tender.

3. Process squash mixture in 2 batches in food processor until
smooth. Return mixture to saucepan. Add remaining can of broth,
nutmeg and pepper. Simmer, uncovered, 5 minutes, stirring
occasionally.*

4. Ladle soup into soup bowls. Place yogurt in pastry bag fitted with
round decorating tip. Pipe onto soup in decorative design, if desired.
Garnish with chives, if desired.   **Makes 6 servings**

*At this point, soup may be covered and refrigerated up to 2 days before
serving. Reheat over medium heat, stirring occasionally.*

Nutrients per Serving (about ¾ cup Bisque [without yogurt]):
Calories 79   Protein 5g
Fat 1g   Carbohydrate 14g
Calories from Fat 9%   Fiber 4g
Saturated Fat <1g   Sodium 107mg
Cholesterol 0mg

Dietary Exchanges: 1 Starch

Broccoli & Potato Chowder

1 can (14½ ounces) fat-free reduced-sodium chicken broth
1 cup sliced leeks
½ cup cubed peeled potato
⅓ cup fresh or frozen corn
1 can (about 4 ounces) mild green chilies, drained
¾ teaspoon paprika
1½ cups broccoli florets
¾ cup evaporated skimmed milk
2 tablespoons all-purpose flour
Jalapeño pepper sauce (optional)

1. Combine broth, leeks, potato, corn, chilies and paprika in medium saucepan. Bring to a boil. Reduce heat; simmer, covered, 10 to 15 minutes or until vegetables are tender. Add broccoli; simmer 3 minutes.

2. Whisk milk into flour in small bowl. Stir into vegetable mixture. Cook, stirring constantly, until soup comes to a boil and thickens slightly. Season to taste with pepper sauce, if desired.

Makes 2 servings

Nutrients per Serving (1 bowl Chowder [½ of total recipe]):

Calories 280	Protein 19g
Fat 1g	Carbohydrate 51g
Calories from Fat 3%	Fiber 5g
Saturated Fat <1g	Sodium 311mg
Cholesterol 3mg	

Dietary Exchanges: 2 Starch, ½ Milk, 3 Vegetable

Summer Minestrone

Nonstick olive oil cooking spray
2 carrots, sliced
1 cup halved green beans
$\frac{1}{2}$ cup sliced celery
$\frac{1}{2}$ cup thinly sliced leek
2 cloves garlic, minced
1 tablespoon fresh sage *or* $\frac{1}{2}$ teaspoon dried sage leaves
1 tablespoon fresh oregano *or* $\frac{1}{2}$ teaspoon dried oregano leaves
3 cans ($14\frac{1}{2}$ ounces each) fat-free reduced-sodium chicken broth
1 zucchini, halved lengthwise and cut into $\frac{1}{2}$-inch-thick slices
1 cup quartered mushrooms
8 ounces cherry tomatoes, halved
$\frac{1}{4}$ cup minced fresh parsley
3 ounces uncooked small rotini
Salt (optional)
Black pepper (optional)
8 teaspoons grated Parmesan cheese

1. Spray large saucepan with cooking spray. Heat over medium heat until hot. Add carrots, green beans, celery, leek, garlic, sage and oregano. Cook and stir 3 to 5 minutes. Add chicken broth; bring to a boil. Reduce heat and simmer about 5 minutes or until vegetables are just crisp-tender.

2. Add zucchini, mushrooms, tomatoes and parsley; bring to a boil. Stir in pasta. Reduce heat and simmer, uncovered, about 8 minutes or until pasta and vegetables are tender. Season to taste with salt and pepper, if desired. Ladle soup into bowls; sprinkle each with 1 teaspoon cheese. **Makes 8 servings**

Nutrients per Serving (1 cup Minestrone [without salt and pepper seasonings]):

Calories 93	Protein 7g
Fat 1g	Carbohydrate 15g
Calories from Fat 9%	Fiber 2g
Saturated Fat <1g	Sodium 96mg
Cholesterol 1mg	

Dietary Exchanges: $\frac{1}{2}$ Starch, 2 Vegetable

Summer Minestrone

Zesty Lentil Stew

    1 cup dried lentils
    2 cups chopped peeled potatoes
    1 can (14½ ounces) fat-free reduced-sodium chicken broth
  1⅔ cups water
  1½ cups chopped seeded tomatoes
    1 can (11½ ounces) no-salt-added spicy vegetable juice
        cocktail
    1 cup chopped onion
  ½ cup chopped carrot
  ½ cup chopped celery
    2 tablespoons chopped fresh basil *or* 2 teaspoons dried basil
        leaves, crushed
    2 tablespoons chopped fresh oregano *or* 2 teaspoons dried
        oregano leaves
    1 to 2 tablespoons finely chopped jalapeño pepper*
  ¼ teaspoon salt

Jalapeño peppers can sting and irritate the skin. Wear rubber gloves when handling peppers and do not touch eyes. Wash hands after handling.

1. Rinse lentils under cold water; drain. Combine lentils, potatoes, broth, water, tomatoes, vegetable juice cocktail, onion, carrot, celery, basil, oregano, jalapeño pepper and salt in 3-quart saucepan.

2. Bring to a boil over high heat. Reduce heat to medium-low. Cover; simmer 45 to 50 minutes or until lentils are tender, stirring occasionally.   **Makes 6 servings**

Nutrients per Serving (1 bowl Stew [⅙ of total recipe]):

Calories 246	Protein 13g
Fat 1g	Carbohydrate 48g
Calories from Fat 3%	Fiber 5g
Saturated Fat <1g	Sodium 413mg
Cholesterol 0mg	

Dietary Exchanges: 2 Starch, 2½ Vegetable, ½ Lean Meat

Zesty Lentil Stew

Roman Spinach Soup

6 cups fat-free reduced-sodium chicken broth
1 cup cholesterol-free egg substitute
¼ cup minced fresh basil
3 tablespoons freshly grated Parmesan cheese
2 tablespoons lemon juice
1 tablespoon minced fresh parsley
¼ teaspoon white pepper
⅛ teaspoon ground nutmeg
8 cups fresh spinach, rinsed, stemmed and chopped
Lemon slices, for garnish (optional)

1. Bring broth to a boil in 4-quart saucepan over medium heat.

2. Beat together egg substitute, basil, Parmesan cheese, lemon juice, parsley, white pepper and nutmeg in medium bowl. Set aside.

3. Stir spinach into broth; simmer 1 minute. Slowly pour egg mixture into broth mixture, whisking constantly so egg threads form. Simmer 2 to 3 minutes or until egg is cooked. Garnish with lemon slices, if desired. Serve immediately.   **Makes 8 servings**

Nutrients per Serving (¾ cup Soup):

Calories 46	Protein 6g
Fat 1g	Carbohydrate 4g
Calories from Fat 22%	Fiber 1g
Saturated Fat 0g	Sodium 153mg
Cholesterol 2mg	

Dietary Exchanges: ½ Vegetable, ½ Lean Meat

Roman Spinach Soup

Chicken Wild Rice Soup

1/3 cup instant nonfat dry milk
2 tablespoons cornstarch
2 teaspoons low sodium instant chicken bouillon
1/4 teaspoon dried onion flakes
1/4 teaspoon dried basil leaves, crushed
1/4 teaspoon dried thyme leaves, crushed
1/8 teaspoon ground pepper
4 cups low sodium chicken broth, divided
1/2 cup sliced celery
1/2 cup sliced carrots
1/2 cup chopped onion
2 cups cooked wild rice
1 cup cooked cubed chicken breasts

In small bowl, combine dry milk, cornstarch, bouillon, onion flakes, basil, thyme and pepper. Stir in small amount of chicken broth; set aside. In large saucepan, combine remaining broth, celery, carrots and onion. Cook until vegetables are crisp-tender. Gradually add dry milk mixture. Stir in wild rice and chicken. Simmer 5 to 10 minutes.

Makes 8 servings

Favorite recipe from **Minnesota Cultivated Wild Rice Council**

Nutrients per Serving (1 bowl Soup [1/8 of total recipe]):

Calories 103	Protein 8g
Fat 1g	Carbohydrate 15g
Calories from Fat 10%	Fiber 1g
Saturated Fat <1g	Sodium 70mg
Cholesterol 13mg	

Dietary Exchanges: 1 Starch, 1/2 Lean Meat

Chilled Roasted Red Pepper Soup

3 Roasted Red Bell Peppers (recipe follows)
3 cups vegetable broth
1 cup diced onions
1 cup water
1 tablespoon chopped garlic
1 bay leaf
$\frac{1}{2}$ teaspoon celery seeds
$\frac{1}{2}$ teaspoon black pepper
2 dashes hot pepper sauce
   Plain nonfat yogurt, for garnish (optional)

1. Place roasted peppers and all remaining ingredients in medium saucepan. Cover; cook over medium heat 45 minutes. Remove bay leaf; discard. Remove saucepan from heat. Let soup cool, uncovered, about 15 minutes. Add soup to food processor or blender; blend until smooth.

2. Chill soup 3 hours in refrigerator or overnight before serving. Top with yogurt dollop, if desired.   **Makes 6 servings**

Roasted Red Bell Peppers: Preheat oven to 400°F. Place peppers on baking sheet; roast about 30 minutes or until charred, turning every 10 minutes. Remove peppers from oven. Place in large resealable plastic food storage bag. Let stand 15 minutes. Remove peppers. Gently peel charred skin from peppers; discard skin. Cut peppers into quarters. Remove seeds and ribs; discard.

Nutrients per Serving ($\frac{3}{4}$ cup Soup [without yogurt]):

Calories 45	Protein 1g
Fat <1g	Carbohydrate 9g
Calories from Fat 9%	Fiber 2g
Saturated Fat <1g	Sodium 233mg
Cholesterol 0mg	

Dietary Exchanges: 2 Vegetable

chapter four

Salads

Black Bean Mexicali Salad

½ cup chopped red or yellow onion, divided
1 can (15 ounces) black beans, rinsed and drained
1 cup fresh or thawed frozen corn
2 large Roasted Red Bell Peppers (page 63), cut into thin strips
    or coarsely chopped
⅓ cup mild chipotle or regular salsa
2 tablespoons cider vinegar
½ cup (2 ounces) part-skim mozzarella cheese, cut into ¼-inch
    cubes

1. Reserve 1 tablespoon onion. Combine remaining onion, beans, corn, bell peppers, salsa and vinegar in medium bowl. Toss until well blended. Let stand 15 minutes.

2. Just before serving, fold all but 2 tablespoons cheese into salad. Top with reserved 2 tablespoons cheese and 1 tablespoon onion.

Makes 7 servings

Nutrients per Serving (½ cup Salad):

Calories 124	Protein 7g
Fat 2g	Carbohydrate 22g
Calories from Fat 13%	Fiber 5g
Saturated Fat 1g	Sodium 278mg
Cholesterol 5mg	

Dietary Exchanges: 1½ Starch, ½ Lean Meat

Black Bean Mexicali Salad

Cucumber Tomato Salad

½ cup rice vinegar*
3 tablespoons EQUAL® SPOONFUL**
3 cups unpeeled ¼-inch-thick sliced cucumbers, quartered
(about 2 medium)
2 cups chopped tomato (about 1 large)
½ cup chopped red onion
Salt and pepper to taste

Distilled white vinegar may be substituted for rice vinegar.

**May substitute 4½ packets Equal® sweetener.*

• Combine vinegar and Equal®. Add cucumbers, tomato and onion. Season to taste with salt and pepper; mix well. Refrigerate, covered, at least 30 minutes before serving. **Makes 6 servings**

Nutrients per Serving (⅙ of total recipe [without salt and pepper seasoning]):

Calories 26	Protein 1g
Fat 0g	Carbohydrate 6g
Calories from Fat 0%	Fiber 1g
Saturated Fat 0g	Sodium 7mg
Cholesterol 0mg	

Dietary Exchanges: 1 Vegetable

Cucumber Tomato Salad

Jerk Turkey Salad

  6 ounces turkey breast tenderloin
1½ teaspoons Caribbean jerk seasoning
  4 cups packaged mixed salad greens
  ¾ cup sliced peeled cucumber
  ⅔ cup chopped fresh pineapple
  ⅔ cup quartered strawberries or whole raspberries
  ½ cup slivered peeled jicama or sliced celery
  1 green onion, sliced
  ¼ cup lime juice
  3 tablespoons honey

1. Prepare grill for direct grilling. Rub turkey with jerk seasoning.

2. Grill turkey over medium coals 15 to 20 minutes or until turkey is no longer pink in center and juices run clear, turning once. Remove from grill and cool.

3. Cut turkey into bite-size pieces. Combine greens, turkey, cucumber, pineapple, strawberries, jicama and green onion.

4. Combine lime juice and honey. Drizzle over salad; toss to coat. Serve immediately.   **Makes 2 servings**

Nutrients per Serving (½ of total recipe):

Calories 265	Protein 17g
Fat 2g	Carbohydrate 48g
Calories from Fat 6%	Fiber 6g
Saturated Fat 1g	Sodium 356mg
Cholesterol 34mg	

Dietary Exchanges: 2 Fruit, 4 Vegetable, 1½ Lean Meat

Jerk Turkey Salad

Fresh Green Salad with Orange Segments and Fat-Free Honey Dressing

$\frac{1}{4}$ cup water
$\frac{1}{4}$ cup white wine vinegar with tarragon or red wine vinegar
$\frac{1}{4}$ cup honey
2 heads butter lettuce
1 head radicchio, leaves separated
2 oranges, peeled and separated into segments

Combine water, vinegar and honey in small jar; cover and shake to mix ingredients. Arrange lettuce and radicchio on 6 salad plates. Divide orange segments among salad plates; drizzle each with dressing.   **Makes 6 servings**

Favorite recipe from **National Honey Board**

Nutrients per Serving ($\frac{1}{6}$ of total recipe):

Calories 75	Protein 1g
Fat <1g	Carbohydrate 18g
Calories from Fat 2%	Fiber 2g
Saturated Fat <1g	Sodium 5mg
Cholesterol 0mg	

Dietary Exchanges: 1 Fruit, 1 Vegetable

sh Green Salad with Orange Segments and Fat-Free Honey Dressing

Santa Fe Grilled Vegetable Salad

2 baby eggplants (6 ounces each), halved
1 medium yellow summer squash, halved
1 medium zucchini, halved
1 medium green bell pepper, cored, seeded and quartered
1 medium red bell pepper, cored, seeded and quartered
1 small onion, peeled and halved
½ cup orange juice
2 tablespoons lime juice
1 tablespoon olive oil
2 cloves garlic, minced
1 teaspoon dried oregano leaves
¼ teaspoon salt
¼ teaspoon ground red pepper
¼ teaspoon black pepper
2 tablespoons chopped fresh cilantro

1. Combine all ingredients except cilantro in large bowl; toss to coat.

2. Spray grid with nonstick cooking spray. Prepare grill for direct grilling. Place vegetables on grill, 2 to 3 inches from hot coals; reserve marinade. Grill 3 to 4 minutes per side or until tender and lightly charred. Remove from grill; cool 10 minutes. Or, place vegetables on rack of broiler pan coated with nonstick cooking spray; reserve marinade. Broil 2 to 3 inches from heat 3 to 4 minutes per side or until tender. Remove from heat; cool 10 minutes.

3. Remove peel from eggplant, if desired. Cut vegetables into bite-size pieces; return to marinade. Stir in cilantro; toss to coat.

Makes 8 servings

Nutrients per Serving (1 cup Salad):

Calories 63	Protein 2g
Fat 2g	Carbohydrate 11g
Calories from Fat 27%	Fiber 1g
Saturated Fat <1g	Sodium 70mg
Cholesterol <1mg	

Dietary Exchanges: 2 Vegetable, ½ Fat

Santa Fe Grilled Vegetable Salad

Skinny Waldorf Salad

2 cups chopped cored Red Delicious apples
1 cup chopped celery
1 cup cubed cooked boneless skinless chicken breast
$\frac{1}{4}$ cup chopped green onions
3 tablespoons lemon nonfat yogurt
2 teaspoons fat-free mayonnaise
1 teaspoon toasted poppy seeds
$\frac{1}{4}$ teaspoon salt
   Dash black pepper

1. Combine apples, celery, chicken and green onions in large bowl; set aside.

2. For dressing, combine yogurt, mayonnaise, poppy seeds, salt and pepper in small bowl. Pour over apple mixture; toss to coat. Refrigerate, covered, at least 1 hour to allow flavors to blend.

Makes 4 servings

Nutrients per Serving ($\frac{1}{4}$ of total recipe):

Calories 95	Protein 9g
Fat 1g	Carbohydrate 12g
Calories from Fat 13%	Fiber 2g
Saturated Fat <1g	Sodium 205mg
Cholesterol 22mg	

Dietary Exchanges: $\frac{1}{2}$ Fruit, $\frac{1}{2}$ Vegetable, 1 Lean Meat

Italian Bread Salad

  3 slices (½-inch-thick) day-old whole wheat bread
 ½ cup low-fat buttermilk
  1 small clove garlic, minced
  1 tablespoon minced fresh dill *or* 1 teaspoon dried dill weed
1½ teaspoons onion powder
 ¼ teaspoon black pepper
  1 small cucumber, peeled
  2 large tomatoes, cored and cut into 1-inch cubes
  1 small rib celery, thinly sliced
  2 tablespoons minced fresh parsley
 ⅛ teaspoon salt

1. Preheat oven to 400°F. Cut bread into 1-inch pieces. Place on baking sheet; bake 5 to 7 minutes or until lightly toasted and dry, stirring occasionally. Remove from pan; cool.

2. For dressing, combine buttermilk, garlic, dill, onion powder and pepper in small jar with tight-fitting lid; shake well. Let stand 15 minutes to allow flavors to blend.

3. Cut cucumber in half lengthwise; remove seeds and thinly slice each half. Place in large bowl; add tomatoes, celery and parsley. Sprinkle with salt; toss well. Just before serving, toss toasted bread with vegetables. Shake dressing; pour over salad and toss to coat. Serve immediately. **Makes 4 servings**

Nutrients per Serving (¼ of total recipe):

Calories 92	Protein 4g
Fat 2g	Carbohydrate 17g
Calories from Fat 14%	Fiber 1g
Saturated Fat <1g	Sodium 220mg
Cholesterol 1mg	

Dietary Exchanges: 1 Starch, ½ Vegetable

Ginger Shrimp Salad

1 package (10 ounces) DOLE® French Salad Blend or Italian
    Salad Blend
6 ounces cooked shelled and deveined medium shrimp or
    cooked tiny shrimp
1 can (11 or 15 ounces) DOLE® Mandarin Oranges, drained
1 medium DOLE® Red, Yellow or Green Bell Pepper, cut into
    2-inch strips
$\frac{1}{3}$ cup fat free or reduced fat mayonnaise
$\frac{1}{3}$ cup DOLE® Pineapple Juice
2 teaspoons finely chopped fresh ginger *or* $\frac{1}{4}$ teaspoon
    ground ginger

• Toss salad blend, shrimp, mandarin oranges and bell pepper in
large serving bowl.

• Stir mayonnaise, juice and ginger in small bowl. Add to salad; toss to
evenly coat.   **Makes 3 servings**

Prep Time: 20 minutes

Nutrients per Serving ($\frac{1}{3}$ of total recipe):

Calories 156	Protein 14g
Fat 1g	Carbohydrate 22g
Calories from Fat 4%	Fiber 3g
Saturated Fat <1g	Sodium 358mg
Cholesterol 111mg	

Dietary Exchanges: 1 Fruit, 1 Vegetable, 2 Lean Meat

Ginger Shrimp Salad

Caribbean Cole Slaw

Orange-Mango Dressing (recipe follows)
8 cups shredded green cabbage
1½ large mangoes, peeled, pitted and diced
½ medium red bell pepper, thinly sliced
½ medium yellow bell pepper, thinly sliced
6 green onions, thinly sliced
¼ cup chopped fresh cilantro

1. Prepare Orange-Mango Dressing.

2. Combine cabbage, mangoes, bell peppers, green onions and cilantro in large bowl; stir gently to mix. Add Orange-Mango Dressing; toss gently to coat. Serve, or store in refrigerator up to 1 day.

Makes 12 servings

Orange-Mango Dressing

½ mango, peeled, pitted and cubed
1 carton (6 ounces) plain nonfat yogurt
¼ cup frozen orange juice concentrate
3 tablespoons lime juice
½ to 1 jalapeño pepper,* stemmed, seeded and minced
1 teaspoon finely minced fresh ginger

*Jalapeño peppers can sting and irritate the skin. Wear rubber gloves when handling peppers and do not touch eyes. Wash hands after handling.

Place mango in food processor; process until smooth. Add remaining ingredients; process until smooth. **Makes 12 servings**

Nutrients per Serving (¹⁄₁₂ of total recipe):

Calories 57	Protein 2g
Fat <1g	Carbohydrate 14g
Calories from Fat 4%	Fiber 2g
Saturated Fat <1g	Sodium 26mg
Cholesterol <1mg	

Dietary Exchanges: ½ Fruit, 1 Vegetable

Caribbean Cole Slaw

Gazpacho Salad

1½ cups peeled and coarsely chopped tomatoes*
1 cup peeled, seeded and diced cucumber
¾ cup chopped onion
½ cup chopped red bell pepper
½ cup fresh or frozen corn kernels, cooked and drained
1 tablespoon lime juice
1 tablespoon red wine vinegar
2 teaspoons water
1 teaspoon minced fresh garlic
1 teaspoon extra-virgin olive oil
¼ teaspoon salt
¼ teaspoon black pepper
   Dash ground red pepper
1 medium head romaine lettuce, torn into bite-size pieces
1 cup peeled and diced jicama
½ cup fresh cilantro sprigs

To peel tomatoes easily, blanch in boiling water 30 seconds. Immediately transfer to bowl of cold water; then peel.

1. Combine tomatoes, cucumber, onion, bell pepper and corn in large bowl. Combine lime juice, vinegar, water, garlic, oil, salt, black pepper and ground red pepper in small bowl; whisk until well blended. Pour over tomato mixture; toss to coat. Cover and refrigerate several hours to allow flavors to blend.

2. Toss together lettuce, jicama and cilantro in another large bowl. Divide lettuce mixture evenly among 6 bowls. Place ⅔ cup chilled tomato mixture on top of each bed of lettuce, spreading to edges.

Makes 6 servings

Nutrients per Serving (⅙ of total recipe):

Calories 71	Protein 3g
Fat 1g	Carbohydrate 14g
Calories from Fat 14%	Fiber 3g
Saturated Fat <1g	Sodium 105mg
Cholesterol 0mg	

Dietary Exchanges: 3 Vegetable

Gazpacho Salad

Thai Beef Salad

½ beef flank steak (about 8 ounces)
¼ cup reduced-sodium soy sauce
2 jalapeño peppers,* finely chopped
2 tablespoons packed brown sugar
1 clove garlic, minced
½ cup lime juice
6 green onions, thinly sliced
4 carrots, diagonally cut into thin slices
½ cup finely chopped fresh cilantro
4 romaine lettuce leaves
    Chives and radish flowers, for garnish (optional)

Jalapeño peppers can sting and irritate the skin. Wear rubber gloves when handling peppers and do not touch eyes. Wash hands after handling.

1. Place flank steak in resealable plastic food storage bag. Combine soy sauce, jalapeños, brown sugar and garlic in small bowl; mix well. Pour mixture over flank steak. Close bag securely; turn to coat steak. Marinate in refrigerator 2 hours.

2. Preheat broiler. Drain steak; discard marinade. Place steak on rack of broiler pan. Broil 4 inches from heat 13 to 18 minutes for medium-rare to medium or until desired doneness, turning once. Remove from heat; let stand 15 minutes.

3. Thinly slice steak across grain. Toss with lime juice, green onions, carrots and cilantro in large bowl. Serve salad immediately on lettuce leaves. Garnish with chives and radish flowers, if desired.

Makes 4 servings

Nutrients per Serving (1 cup Salad with 1 lettuce leaf):

Calories 141	Protein 13g
Fat 4g	Carbohydrate 14g
Calories from Fat 26%	Fiber 3g
Saturated Fat 2g	Sodium 238mg
Cholesterol 27mg	

Dietary Exchanges: 2 Vegetable, 1½ Lean Meat

Thai Beef Salad

chapter five

Meats

Spicy Caribbean Pork Medallions

6 ounces pork tenderloin
1 teaspoon Caribbean jerk seasoning
   Nonstick olive oil cooking spray
⅓ cup pineapple juice
1 teaspoon brown mustard
½ teaspoon cornstarch

1. Cut tenderloin into ½-inch-thick slices. Place each slice between 2 pieces of plastic wrap. Pound to ¼-inch thickness. Rub both sides of pork pieces with jerk seasoning.

2. Lightly spray large nonstick skillet with cooking spray; heat over medium heat until hot. Add pork. Cook 2 to 3 minutes or until no longer pink, turning once. Remove from skillet. Keep warm.

3. Stir together pineapple juice, mustard and cornstarch until smooth. Add to skillet. Cook and stir over medium heat until mixture comes to a boil and thickens slightly. Spoon over pork.

Makes 2 servings

Nutrients per Serving (½ of total recipe):

Calories 134	Protein 18g
Fat 3g	Carbohydrate 7g
Calories from Fat 23%	Fiber <1g
Saturated Fat 1g	Sodium 319mg
Cholesterol 49mg	

Dietary Exchanges: ½ Fruit, 2 Lean Meat

Spicy Caribbean Pork Medallions

Sirloin with Sweet Caramelized Onions

Nonstick cooking spray
1 medium onion, very thinly sliced
1 boneless beef top sirloin steak (about 1 pound)
¼ cup water
2 tablespoons Worcestershire sauce
1 tablespoon sugar

1. Lightly coat 12-inch skillet with cooking spray; heat over high heat until hot. Add onion; cook and stir 4 minutes or until browned. Remove from skillet; set aside. Wipe out skillet with paper towel.

2. Coat same skillet with cooking spray; heat over medium heat until hot. Add beef; cook 10 to 13 minutes for medium-rare to medium, turning once. Remove from heat and transfer to cutting board; let stand 3 minutes before slicing.

3. Meanwhile, return skillet to high heat until hot; add onion, water, Worcestershire sauce and sugar. Cook 30 to 45 seconds or until most liquid has evaporated.

4. Thinly slice beef on the diagonal and serve with onions.

Makes 4 servings

Nutrients per Serving (¼ of total recipe):

Calories 159	Protein 21g
Fat 5g	Carbohydrate 7g
Calories from Fat 28%	Fiber 1g
Saturated Fat 2g	Sodium 118mg
Cholesterol 60mg	

Dietary Exchanges: 1 Vegetable, 3 Lean Meat

Sirloin with Sweet Caramelized Onions

Thai-Style Pork Kabobs

⅓ cup reduced-sodium soy sauce
2 tablespoons *each* water and fresh lime juice
2 teaspoons hot chili oil*
2 cloves garlic, minced
1 teaspoon minced fresh ginger
¾ pound well-trimmed pork tenderloin
1 medium red or yellow bell pepper, cut into ½-inch pieces
1 medium red or sweet onion, cut into ½-inch chunks
2 cups hot cooked rice

If hot chili oil is not available, combine 2 teaspoons vegetable oil and ½ teaspoon red pepper flakes in small microwavable cup. Microwave at HIGH 30 to 45 seconds. Let stand 5 minutes to allow flavor to develop.

1. Combine soy sauce, water, lime juice, chili oil, garlic and ginger in medium bowl. Reserve ⅓ cup mixture for dipping sauce; set aside.

2. Cut pork tenderloin lengthwise in half; cut crosswise into 4-inch-thick slices. Cut slices into ½-inch strips. Add to bowl with soy sauce mixture; toss to coat. Cover; refrigerate at least 30 minutes or up to 2 hours, turning once.

3. Spray grid with nonstick cooking spray. Prepare grill for direct grilling.

4. Remove pork from marinade; discard marinade. Alternately weave pork strips and thread bell pepper and onion chunks onto 8 (8- to 10-inch) metal skewers.

5. Grill, covered, over medium-hot coals 6 to 8 minutes or until pork is no longer pink in center, turning halfway through grilling time. Serve with rice and reserved ⅓ cup dipping sauce.

Makes 4 servings

Nutrients per Serving (2 Kabobs with ½ cup rice and about
1 tablespoon plus 1 teaspoon dipping sauce):

Calories 248	Protein 22g
Fat 4g	Carbohydrate 30g
Calories from Fat 16%	Fiber 2g
Saturated Fat 1g	Sodium 271mg
Cholesterol 49mg	

Dietary Exchanges: 1½ Starch, 1 Vegetable, 2 Lean Meat

Thai-Style Pork Kabobs

Chili Beef & Red Pepper Fajitas with Chipotle Salsa

6 ounces boneless beef top sirloin steak, thinly sliced
½ lime
1½ teaspoons chili powder
½ teaspoon ground cumin
½ cup diced plum tomatoes
¼ cup mild picante sauce
½ canned chipotle chili pepper in adobo sauce
Nonstick cooking spray
½ cup sliced onion
½ medium red bell pepper, cut into thin strips
2 (10-inch) fat-free flour tortillas, warmed
¼ cup fat-free sour cream
2 tablespoons chopped fresh cilantro leaves (optional)

1. Place steak on plate. Squeeze lime juice over steak; sprinkle with chili powder and cumin. Coat well; let stand 10 minutes.

2. Meanwhile, prepare salsa. Combine tomatoes and picante sauce in small bowl. Place chipotle on small plate. Using fork, mash completely. Stir mashed chipotle into tomato mixture. Set aside.

3. Coat 12-inch skillet with cooking spray. Heat over high heat until hot. Add onion and bell pepper; cook and stir 3 minutes or until edges begin to blacken. Remove from skillet. Lightly spray skillet with cooking spray. Add beef; stir-fry 1 minute. Return onion and bell pepper to skillet; cook 1 minute longer.

4. Place ½ of beef mixture in center of each tortilla; fold sides of tortilla over filling. Top each fajita with ¼ cup salsa, 2 tablespoons sour cream and cilantro, if desired.   **Makes 2 servings**

Nutrients per Serving (1 Fajita with ¼ cup Salsa and 2 tablespoons fat-free sour cream [without garnish]):

Calories 245	Protein 21g
Fat 4g	Carbohydrate 31g
Calories from Fat 16%	Fiber 9g
Saturated Fat 2g	Sodium 530mg
Cholesterol 45mg	

Dietary Exchanges: 1½ Starch, 1 Vegetable, 2 Lean Meat

Chili Beef & Red Pepper Fajita with Chipotle Salsa

Grilled Pork Tenderloin Medallions

Pepper & Herb Rub
 1 tablespoon garlic salt
 1 tablespoon dried basil leaves
 1 tablespoon dried thyme leaves
 1½ teaspoons dried rosemary leaves
 1½ teaspoons cracked black pepper
 1 teaspoon paprika
Pork
 2 tablespoons Pepper & Herb Rub
 12 pork tenderloin medallions (about 1 pound)
  Nonstick olive oil cooking spray

1. For rub, combine salt, basil, thyme, rosemary, pepper and paprika in small jar or resealable plastic food storage bag. Store in cool dry place up to 3 months.

2. Prepare grill for direct grilling. Sprinkle rub evenly over both sides of pork; press rub lightly into pork. Spray pork with cooking spray.

3. Place pork on grid over medium-hot coals. Grill, uncovered, 4 to 5 minutes per side or until pork is no longer pink in center.

Makes 4 servings

Serving Suggestion: Serve with steamed red potatoes and bell peppers.

Nutrients per Serving (3 Pork Medallions):

Calories 145	Protein 24g
Fat 4g	Carbohydrate 2g
Calories from Fat 27%	Fiber 1g
Saturated Fat 1g	Sodium 528mg
Cholesterol 66mg	

Dietary Exchanges: 3 Lean Meat

Grilled Pork Tenderloin Medallions

Italian-Style Meat Loaf

1 can (6 ounces) no-salt-added tomato paste
$\frac{1}{2}$ cup dry red wine plus $\frac{1}{2}$ cup water *or* 1 cup water
1 teaspoon minced garlic
$\frac{1}{2}$ teaspoon dried basil leaves
$\frac{1}{2}$ teaspoon dried oregano leaves
$\frac{1}{4}$ teaspoon salt
$\frac{3}{4}$ pound 95% lean ground beef
$\frac{3}{4}$ pound 93% lean ground turkey
1 cup fresh whole wheat bread crumbs (2 slices whole wheat bread)
$\frac{1}{2}$ cup shredded zucchini
$\frac{1}{4}$ cup cholesterol-free egg substitute *or* 2 egg whites

1. Preheat oven to 350°F. Combine tomato paste, wine, water, garlic, basil, oregano and salt in small saucepan. Bring to a boil. Reduce heat to low; simmer, uncovered, 15 minutes. Remove from heat.

2. Combine beef, turkey, bread crumbs, zucchini, egg substitute and $\frac{1}{2}$ cup tomato mixture in large bowl; mix well. Shape into loaf; place in ungreased 9×5×3-inch loaf pan. Bake 45 minutes. Discard any drippings. Pour $\frac{1}{2}$ cup remaining tomato mixture over top of loaf. Bake additional 15 minutes. Place on serving platter. Cool 10 minutes before cutting into 8 slices. Garnish as desired. **Makes 8 servings**

Nutrients per Serving (1 slice [$\frac{1}{8}$ of Meat Loaf]):
Calories 144
Protein 19g
Fat 2g
Carbohydrate 7g
Calories from Fat 11%
Fiber 1g
Saturated Fat 1g
Sodium 171mg
Cholesterol 41mg

Dietary Exchanges: $\frac{1}{2}$ Starch, 2 Lean Meat

Italian-Style Meat Loaf

Mandarin Pork Stir-Fry

1 1/2 cups DOLE® Pineapple Orange or Pineapple Juice, divided
    Vegetable cooking spray
12 ounces lean pork tenderloin, chicken breast or turkey
    tenderloin, cut into thin strips
1 tablespoon finely chopped fresh ginger *or* 1/2 teaspoon
    ground ginger
2 cups DOLE® Shredded Carrots
1/2 cup chopped DOLE® Pitted Prunes or Chopped Dates
4 green onions, cut into 1-inch pieces
2 tablespoons low-sodium soy sauce
1 teaspoon cornstarch

• Heat 2 tablespoons juice over medium-high heat in large nonstick skillet sprayed with vegetable cooking spray until juice bubbles.

• Add pork and ginger; cook and stir 3 minutes or until pork is no longer pink. Remove pork from skillet.

• Heat 3 more tablespoons juice in skillet; add carrots, prunes and green onions. Cook and stir 3 minutes.

• Stir soy sauce and cornstarch into remaining juice; add to carrot mixture. Stir in pork; cover and cook 2 minutes until heated through.

Makes 4 servings

Prep Time: 15 minutes
Cook Time: 15 minutes

Nutrients per Serving (1/4 of total recipe):

Calories 231	Protein 21g
Fat 3g	Carbohydrate 31g
Calories from Fat 12%	Fiber 3g
Saturated Fat 1g	Sodium 323mg
Cholesterol 49mg	

Dietary Exchanges: 1 1/2 Fruit, 1 Vegetable, 2 Lean Meat

Chunky Joes

    Nonstick cooking spray
    1 pound 95% lean ground beef
    1½ cups finely chopped green bell pepper
    1 can (14½ ounces) stewed tomatoes
    ¼ cup water
    2 tablespoons tomato paste
    1 tablespoon chili powder
    1 tablespoon Worcestershire sauce
    1 packet sugar substitute
    1 teaspoon ground cumin, divided
    6 hamburger buns, warmed

1. Lightly coat 12-inch skillet with cooking spray. Heat over high heat until hot. Add beef; cook and stir 3 minutes or until no longer pink. Drain on paper towels; set aside. Wipe out skillet with paper towel.

2. Coat skillet with cooking spray; heat over medium-high heat until hot. Add bell pepper; cook and stir 4 minutes or until just tender. Add tomatoes, water, tomato paste, chili powder, Worcestershire sauce, sugar substitute and ½ teaspoon cumin. Bring to a boil. Reduce heat; simmer, covered, 20 minutes or until thickened.

3. Remove from heat. Stir in remaining ½ teaspoon cumin. If thicker consistency is desired, cook 5 minutes longer, uncovered, stirring frequently.

4. Spoon ½ cup mixture onto each bun.   **Makes 6 servings**

Nutrients per Serving (1 Chunky Joe sandwich):

Calories 251	Protein 19g
Fat 5g	Carbohydrate 32g
Calories from Fat 18%	Fiber 4g
Saturated Fat 1g	Sodium 505mg
Cholesterol 39mg	

Dietary Exchanges: 2 Starch, 1 Vegetable, 2 Lean Meat

Lemon-Capered Pork Tenderloin

1 boneless pork tenderloin (about 1½ pounds)
1 tablespoon crushed capers
1 teaspoon dried rosemary leaves, crushed
⅛ teaspoon black pepper
1 cup water
¼ cup lemon juice

1. Preheat oven to 350°F. Trim fat from tenderloin; discard. Set tenderloin aside.

2. Combine capers, rosemary and black pepper in small bowl. Rub mixture over tenderloin. Place tenderloin in shallow roasting pan. Pour water and lemon juice over tenderloin.

3. Bake, uncovered, 1 hour or until thermometer inserted into thickest part of tenderloin registers 160°F. Remove from oven; cover with foil. Allow to stand 10 minutes. Cut into slices before serving. Garnish as desired.   **Makes 8 servings**

Nutrients per Serving (⅛ of total recipe [without garnish]):

Calories 114	Protein 19g
Fat 3g	Carbohydrate <1g
Calories from Fat 28%	Fiber <1g
Saturated Fat 1g	Sodium 59mg
Cholesterol 45mg	

Dietary Exchanges: 2 Lean Meat

Lemon-Capered Pork Tenderloin

Fajita Stuffed Shells

¼ cup fresh lime juice
1 clove garlic, minced
½ teaspoon dried oregano leaves
¼ teaspoon ground cumin
½ boneless beef top round or beef flank steak (about 3 ounces)
1 medium green bell pepper, halved and seeded
1 medium onion, cut in half
12 uncooked jumbo pasta shells (about 6 ounces)
½ cup reduced-fat sour cream
2 tablespoons shredded reduced-fat Cheddar cheese
1 tablespoon minced fresh cilantro
⅔ cup chunky salsa
2 cups shredded leaf lettuce

1. Combine lime juice, garlic, oregano and cumin in shallow nonmetallic dish. Add steak, bell pepper and onion. Cover; refrigerate 8 hours or overnight.

2. Preheat oven to 350°F. Cook pasta shells according to package directions, omitting salt. Drain and rinse well under cold water; set aside.

3. Grill or broil steak and vegetables over medium heat 6 to 8 minutes for medium or until desired doneness, turning once. Cool slightly. Cut steak into thin slices. Chop vegetables. Place steak slices and vegetables in medium bowl. Stir in sour cream, Cheddar cheese and cilantro. Stuff shells evenly with meat mixture, mounding slightly.

4. Arrange shells in 8-inch baking dish. Pour salsa over filled shells. Cover with foil; bake 15 minutes or until heated through. Divide lettuce evenly among 4 plates; arrange 3 shells on each plate.

Makes 4 servings

Nutrients per Serving (3 Stuffed Shells with ½ cup lettuce):

Calories 265	Protein 19g
Fat 5g	Carbohydrate 36g
Calories from Fat 16%	Fiber 3g
Saturated Fat 2g	Sodium 341mg
Cholesterol 33mg	

Dietary Exchanges: 2 Starch, 1 Vegetable, 1½ Lean Meat

Fajita Stuffed Shells

Blackberry-Glazed Pork Medallions

⅓ cup no-sugar-added seedless blackberry spread
4½ teaspoons red wine vinegar
1 tablespoon sugar
¼ teaspoon red pepper flakes
  Nonstick cooking spray
1 teaspoon vegetable oil
1 pound pork tenderloin, cut into ¼-inch-thick slices
¼ teaspoon salt, divided
¼ teaspoon dried thyme leaves, divided

1. Whisk blackberry spread, vinegar, sugar and red pepper flakes in small bowl until blended; set aside.

2. Heat large nonstick skillet over medium-high heat until hot. Coat skillet with cooking spray; add oil and tilt skillet to coat bottom. Add half of pork slices; sprinkle with half of salt and half of thyme. Cook 2 minutes; turn and cook 1 minute on other side. Remove pork from skillet; set aside. Repeat with remaining pork, salt and thyme.

3. Add blackberry mixture to skillet; bring to a boil over high heat. Add reserved pork slices, discarding any accumulated juices. Cook about 4 minutes, turning constantly, until pork is richly glazed.

Makes 4 servings

Nutrients per Serving (¼ of total recipe):

Calories 186	Protein 23g
Fat 5g	Carbohydrate 10g
Calories from Fat 26%	Fiber <1g
Saturated Fat 2g	Sodium 219mg
Cholesterol 66mg	

Dietary Exchanges: ½ Fruit, 3 Lean Meat

Blackberry-Glazed Pork Medallions

chapter six

Poultry

Spiced Turkey with Fruit Salsa

6 ounces turkey breast tenderloin
2 teaspoons lime juice
1 teaspoon mesquite seasoning blend or ground cumin
$\frac{1}{2}$ cup frozen pitted sweet cherries, thawed and cut into halves*
$\frac{1}{4}$ cup chunky salsa

Drained canned sweet cherries can be substituted for frozen cherries.

1. Prepare grill for direct grilling. Brush both sides of turkey with lime juice. Sprinkle with mesquite seasoning.

2. Grill turkey over medium coals 15 to 20 minutes or until turkey is no longer pink in center and juices run clear, turning once.

3. Meanwhile, stir together cherries and salsa.

4. Thinly slice turkey. Spoon salsa mixture over turkey.

Makes 2 servings

Nutrients per Serving ($\frac{1}{2}$ of total recipe):

Calories 125	Protein 16g
Fat 2g	Carbohydrate 11g
Calories from Fat 13%	Fiber 2g
Saturated Fat 1g	Sodium 264mg
Cholesterol 34mg	

Dietary Exchanges: $\frac{1}{2}$ Fruit, 2 Lean Meat

Spiced Turkey with Fruit Salsa

Chicken Marsala

4 BUTTERBALL® Boneless Skinless Chicken Breast Fillets
3 cups sliced fresh mushrooms
2 tablespoons sliced green onion
2 tablespoons water
$\frac{1}{4}$ teaspoon salt
$\frac{1}{4}$ cup dry Marsala wine
1 teaspoon cornstarch

Flatten chicken fillets between two pieces of plastic wrap. Spray nonstick skillet with nonstick cooking spray; heat over medium heat until hot. Add chicken; cook 2 to 3 minutes on each side or until no longer pink in center. Transfer to platter; keep warm. Add mushrooms, onion, water and salt to skillet. Cook 3 minutes or until most of the liquid has evaporated. Combine wine and cornstarch in small bowl; add to skillet. Heat, stirring constantly, until thickened. Spoon over warm chicken. **Makes 4 servings**

Preparation Time: 15 to 20 minutes

Nutrients per Serving ($\frac{1}{4}$ of total recipe):

Calories 140	Protein 26g
Fat 1g	Carbohydrate 3g
Calories from Fat 4%	Fiber 1g
Saturated Fat 1g	Sodium 390mg
Cholesterol 69mg	

Dietary Exchanges: 3 Lean Meat

Chicken Marsala

Tex-Mex Tostadas

4 (8-inch) fat-free flour tortillas
Nonstick cooking spray
1 green bell pepper, diced
³⁄₄ pound boneless skinless chicken breasts, cut into strips
1¹⁄₂ teaspoons minced garlic
1 teaspoon chili powder
1 teaspoon ground cumin
¹⁄₂ cup chunky salsa, divided
¹⁄₃ cup sliced green onions
1 cup canned fat-free refried beans
1 medium tomato, diced
¹⁄₄ cup fat-free sour cream (optional)

1. Preheat oven to 450°F. Place tortillas on baking sheet; coat both sides with cooking spray. Bake 5 minutes or until lightly browned and crisp. Remove; set aside.

2. Coat large nonstick skillet with cooking spray. Add bell pepper; cook and stir 4 minutes over medium-high heat. Add chicken, garlic, chili powder and cumin; cook and stir 4 minutes or until chicken is no longer pink in center. Add ¹⁄₄ cup salsa and green onions; cook and stir 1 minute. Remove skillet from heat; set aside.

3. Combine refried beans and remaining ¹⁄₄ cup salsa in microwavable bowl. Cook uncovered at HIGH 1¹⁄₂ minutes or until beans are heated through.

4. Spread bean mixture evenly over tortillas. Spoon chicken mixture and tomato over bean mixture. Garnish with sour cream, if desired.

Makes 4 servings

Nutrients per Serving (1 Tostada [¹⁄₄ of total recipe] without sour cream):

Calories 251	Protein 26g
Fat 3g	Carbohydrate 30g
Calories from Fat 9%	Fiber 11g
Saturated Fat 1g	Sodium 707mg
Cholesterol 52mg	

Dietary Exchanges: 2 Starch, 2 Lean Meat

Tex-Mex Tostada

Chicken Roll-Ups

¼ cup fresh lemon juice
1 tablespoon olive oil
¼ teaspoon salt
¼ teaspoon black pepper
4 boneless skinless chicken breasts (about 1 pound)
¼ cup finely chopped fresh Italian parsley
2 tablespoons grated Parmesan cheese
2 tablespoons chopped fresh chives
1 teaspoon finely grated lemon peel
2 large cloves garlic, pressed in garlic press
16 toothpicks, soaked in hot water 15 minutes

1. Combine lemon juice, oil, salt and pepper in 11×7-inch casserole. Pound chicken to ⅜-inch thickness. Place chicken in lemon mixture; turn to coat. Cover; marinate in refrigerator at least 30 minutes.

2. Prepare grill for direct grilling.

3. Combine parsley, cheese, chives, lemon peel and garlic in small bowl. Discard chicken marinade. Spread ¼ of parsley mixture over each chicken breast, to within 1 inch of edge. Starting at narrow end, roll chicken to enclose filling; secure with toothpicks.

4. Grill chicken, covered, over medium-hot coals about 2 minutes on each side or until golden brown. Transfer chicken to low or indirect heat; grill, covered, about 5 minutes or until chicken is no longer pink in center.

5. Remove toothpicks; slice each chicken breast into pieces.

Makes 4 servings

Nutrients per Serving (1 rolled-up chicken breast):

Calories 159	Protein 27g
Fat 4g	Carbohydrate 2g
Calories from Fat 24%	Fiber <1g
Saturated Fat 1g	Sodium 139mg
Cholesterol 69mg	

Dietary Exchanges: 3 Lean Meat

Chicken Roll-Up

90's-Style Slow Cooker Coq au Vin

2 packages BUTTERBALL® Boneless Skinless Chicken Breast
   Fillets
1 pound fresh mushrooms, sliced thick
1 jar (15 ounces) pearl onions, drained
½ cup dry white wine
1 teaspoon thyme leaves
1 bay leaf
1 cup chicken broth
⅓ cup flour
½ cup chopped fresh parsley

Slow Cooker Directions

Place chicken, mushrooms, onions, wine, thyme and bay leaf in slow
cooker. Combine chicken broth and flour; pour into slow cooker.
Cover and cook 5 hours on low setting. Add parsley. Serve over wild
rice pilaf, if desired. **Makes 8 servings**

Note: Remove and discard bay leaf before serving dish.

Prep Time: 30 minutes plus cooking time

Nutrients per Serving (⅛ of total recipe [without wild rice pilaf]):

Calories 175	Protein 23g
Fat 2g	Carbohydrate 15g
Calories from Fat 8%	Fiber 1g
Saturated Fat <1g	Sodium 181mg
Cholesterol 49mg	

Dietary Exchanges: ½ Starch, 1½ Vegetable, 2½ Lean Meat

Grilled Chicken with Extra Spicy Corn and Black Beans

4 tablespoons MRS. DASH® Extra Spicy seasoning, divided
1 cup canned black beans, drained and rinsed
1 cup frozen yellow corn, thawed, cooked and cooled
1 medium red bell pepper, seeded and chopped (optional)
$\frac{1}{2}$ cup finely chopped fresh cilantro
$\frac{1}{4}$ cup finely chopped red onion
2 tablespoons fresh lime juice
4 boneless skinless chicken breast halves (about 1 pound)

At least one hour before grilling chicken, prepare Salsa. Mix 2 tablespoons Mrs. Dash Extra Spicy seasoning, black beans, yellow corn, pepper (if using), cilantro, red onion and fresh lime juice until well blended. Set aside, stirring once or twice. To prepare Chicken, preheat grill to medium-high. Place 2 tablespoons Mrs. Dash Extra Spicy seasoning in a plastic bag. Place chicken in the bag and shake until well coated. Place on grill and cook 5 minutes. Turn and cook additional 5 minutes, or until juices run clear when skewer is inserted. Serve hot with salsa on the side. **Makes 4 servings**

Preparation Time: 10 minutes
Cooking Time: 12 minutes

Nutrients per Serving ($\frac{1}{4}$ of total recipe [without salsa]):

Calories 220	Protein 31g
Fat 2g	Carbohydrate 20g
Calories from Fat 7%	Fiber 4g
Saturated Fat <1g	Sodium 262mg
Cholesterol 66mg	

Dietary Exchanges: 1 Starch, 1 Vegetable, $2\frac{1}{2}$ Lean Meat

Rice and Turkey Skillet Curry

　2 cups water
　1 cup UNCLE BEN'S® ORIGINAL CONVERTED® Brand Rice
　¾ cup (6 ounces) pineapple juice
　⅓ cup diced dried apricots
　¼ cup dried cranberries
　1 teaspoon curry powder
　1½ cups (8 ounces) cooked turkey

1. In large skillet, bring 2 cups water, rice, pineapple juice, apricots, cranberries and curry powder to a boil. Cover; reduce heat and simmer 15 minutes or until rice is tender and liquid is absorbed.

2. Add turkey to rice. Cover and cook over low heat 5 minutes or until turkey is hot. **Makes 4 servings**

Nutrients per Serving (¼ of total recipe):

Calories 256	Protein 20g
Fat 1g	Carbohydrate 43g
Calories from Fat 3%	Fiber 2g
Saturated Fat <1g	Sodium 41mg
Cholesterol 47mg	

Dietary Exchanges: 2 Starch, 1 Fruit, 2 Lean Meat

Rice and Turkey Skillet Curry

Crispy Baked Chicken

8 ounces (1 cup) fat-free French onion dip
½ cup fat-free (skim) milk
1 cup cornflake crumbs
½ cup wheat germ
6 skinless chicken breasts or thighs (about 2 pounds)

1. Preheat oven to 350°F. Spray shallow baking pan with nonstick cooking spray.

2. Place dip in shallow bowl; stir until smooth. Add milk, 1 tablespoon at a time, until pourable consistency is reached.

3. Combine cornflake crumbs and wheat germ on plate.

4. Dip chicken pieces in milk mixture, then roll in cornflake mixture. Place chicken in single layer in prepared pan. Bake 45 to 50 minutes or until juices run clear when chicken is pierced with fork and chicken is no longer pink near bone. **Makes 6 servings**

Nutrients per Serving (1 Crispy Baked Chicken breast):

Calories 253	Protein 35g
Fat 2g	Carbohydrate 22g
Calories from Fat 8%	Fiber 1g
Saturated Fat <1g	Sodium 437mg
Cholesterol 66mg	

Dietary Exchanges: 1½ Starch, 3 Lean Meat

Crispy Baked Chicken

Tuscan Pasta

1 pound boneless skinless chicken breasts, cut into 1-inch
    pieces
2 cans (14½ ounces each) Italian-style stewed tomatoes
1 can (15½ ounces) red kidney beans, rinsed and drained
1 can (15 ounces) tomato sauce
1 medium green bell pepper, chopped
1 cup water
1 jar (4½ ounces) sliced mushrooms, drained
½ cup chopped onion
½ cup chopped celery
4 cloves garlic, minced
1 teaspoon Italian seasoning
6 ounces uncooked thin spaghetti, broken in half

Slow Cooker Directions

1. Place all ingredients except spaghetti in slow cooker. Cover; cook on LOW 4 hours or until vegetables are tender.

2. Turn to HIGH. Stir in spaghetti. Cover; cook 45 minutes or until pasta is tender, stirring after 10 minutes. Garnish with basil and bell pepper strips, if desired. **Makes 8 servings**

Nutrients per Serving (⅛ of total recipe [without garnish]):

Calories 266	Protein 21g
Fat 2g	Carbohydrate 40g
Calories from Fat 6%	Fiber 6g
Saturated Fat 1g	Sodium 814mg
Cholesterol 34mg	

Dietary Exchanges: 2 Starch, 2 Vegetable, 1½ Lean Meat

Tuscan Pasta

Turkey Yakitori

½ teaspoon low sodium chicken bouillon granules
2 tablespoons boiling water
2 tablespoons reduced sodium soy sauce
2 tablespoons dry sherry
1 teaspoon ground ginger
1 garlic clove, minced
2 pounds turkey breast cutlets, cut into 1-inch-wide strips
8 metal skewers (9 inches long)
½ pound fresh whole mushrooms
½ large red bell pepper, cut into 1-inch cubes
½ large green bell pepper, cut into 1-inch cubes

1. Dissolve bouillon in boiling water in small bowl.

2. Combine bouillon mixture, soy sauce, sherry, ginger, garlic and turkey in large resealable plastic bag. Seal bag and turn mixture to coat. Refrigerate 4 hours or overnight. Drain marinade and discard.*

3. Weave turkey strips around mushrooms and pepper cubes on skewers.

4. Remove grill rack from charcoal grill and lightly coat with cooking spray; set aside. Preheat charcoal grill for direct-heat cooking. Grill turkey skewers 4 to 5 minutes or until turkey is no longer pink.

Makes 4 servings

If desired, prepare another recipe of marinade by combining first six ingredients to use as a dipping sauce. DO NOT use any of original marinade as dipping sauce when serving.

Favorite recipe from **National Turkey Federation**

Nutrients per Serving (2 skewers [without additional dipping sauce]):

Calories 288	Protein 58g
Fat 1g	Carbohydrate 7g
Calories from Fat 4%	Fiber 1g
Saturated Fat <1g	Sodium 344mg
Cholesterol 150mg	

Dietary Exchanges: ½ Vegetable, 5 Lean Meat

Caribbean Grilled Turkey

1 package BUTTERBALL® Fresh Boneless Turkey Breast
    Tenderloins
4 green onions
4 cloves garlic
2 tablespoons peach preserves
2 tablespoons fresh lime juice
1 teaspoon salt
1 teaspoon shredded lime peel
1 teaspoon bottled hot sauce
1 teaspoon soy sauce
¼ teaspoon black pepper

Lightly spray unheated grill rack with nonstick cooking spray. Prepare grill for medium-direct-heat cooking. In food processor or blender, process onions, garlic, preserves, lime juice, salt, lime peel, hot sauce, soy sauce and pepper until smooth. Spread over tenderloins. Place tenderloins on rack over medium-hot grill. Grill 20 minutes or until meat is no longer pink, turning frequently for even browning.

Makes 6 servings

Preparation Time: 25 minutes

Nutrients per Serving (⅙ of total recipe):

Calories 88	Protein 14g
Fat <1g	Carbohydrate 7g
Calories from Fat 3%	Fiber <1g
Saturated Fat <1g	Sodium 488mg
Cholesterol 37mg	

Dietary Exchanges: ½ Starch, 1½ Lean Meat

chapter seven

Seafood

Seafood Risotto

1 package (5.2 ounces) rice in creamy sauce (Risotto Milanese
  flavor)
1 package (14 to 16 ounces) frozen fully cooked shrimp
1 box (10 ounces) BIRDS EYE® frozen Mixed Vegetables
2 teaspoons grated Parmesan cheese

• In 4-quart saucepan, prepare rice according to package directions.
Add frozen shrimp and vegetables during last 10 minutes of cooking.

• Sprinkle with cheese.   **Makes 4 servings**

Serving Suggestion: Serve with garlic bread and a tossed green
salad, if desired.

Prep Time: 5 minutes
Cook Time: 15 minutes

Nutrients per Serving ($\frac{1}{4}$ of total recipe):
Calories 303	Protein 28g
Fat 2g	Carbohydrate 39g
Calories from Fat 7%	Fiber 3g
Saturated Fat 1g	Sodium 866mg
Cholesterol 175mg	

Dietary Exchanges: $2\frac{1}{2}$ Starch, 3 Lean Meat

Seafood Risotto

Caribbean Sea Bass with Mango Salsa

4 skinless sea bass fillets (4 ounces each), about 1 inch thick
1 teaspoon Caribbean jerk seasoning
  Nonstick cooking spray
1 ripe mango, peeled, pitted and diced *or* 1 cup diced drained
    bottled mango
2 tablespoons chopped fresh cilantro
2 teaspoons fresh lime juice
1 teaspoon minced fresh or bottled jalapeño pepper*

Jalapeño peppers can sting and irritate the skin. Wear rubber gloves when handling peppers and do not touch eyes. Wash hands after handling.

1. Prepare grill or preheat broiler.

2. Sprinkle fish with seasoning; coat lightly with cooking spray. Grill over medium coals or broil 5 inches from heat 4 to 5 minutes per side or until fish flakes easily when tested with fork.

3. Meanwhile, combine mango, cilantro, lime juice and jalapeño pepper in small bowl; mix well. Serve salsa over fish.

Makes 4 servings

Prep Time: 10 minutes
Cook Time: 8 minutes

Nutrients per Serving (1 fillet with about ¼ cup Mango Salsa):

Calories 146	Protein 21g
Fat 3g	Carbohydrate 9g
Calories from Fat 15%	Fiber 1g
Saturated Fat 1g	Sodium 189mg
Cholesterol 47mg	

Dietary Exchanges: ½ Fruit, 2½ Lean Meat

Caribbean Sea Bass with Mango Salsa

Red Snapper Vera Cruz

4 red snapper fillets (about 1 pound)
¼ cup fresh lime juice
1 tablespoon fresh lemon juice
1 teaspoon chili powder
4 green onions with 4 inches of tops, sliced into ½-inch lengths
1 tomato, coarsely chopped
½ cup chopped Anaheim or green bell pepper
½ cup chopped red bell pepper
   Black pepper

Microwave Directions

1. Place fish in shallow 9- to 10-inch round microwavable baking dish. Combine lime juice, lemon juice and chili powder in small bowl. Pour over fish. Marinate in refrigerator 10 minutes, turning once or twice.

2. Sprinkle green onions, tomato, Anaheim pepper and red bell pepper over fish. Season to taste with black pepper. Cover dish loosely with vented plastic wrap. Microwave at HIGH 5 to 6 minutes or just until fish flakes in center when tested with fork, rotating dish every 2 minutes. Let stand, covered, 4 minutes.   **Makes 4 servings**

Prep and Cook Time: 22 minutes

Nutrients per Serving (1 fillet with about ½ cup salsa):

Calories 144	Protein 24g
Fat 2g	Carbohydrate 7g
Calories from Fat 12%	Fiber 2g
Saturated Fat <1g	Sodium 61mg
Cholesterol 42mg	

Dietary Exchanges: 1 Vegetable, 2½ Lean Meat

Red Snapper Vera Cruz

Baked Cod with Tomatoes and Olives

1 pound cod fillets (about 4 fillets), cut into 2-inch pieces
Salt (optional)
Black pepper (optional)
1 can (14½ ounces) diced Italian-style tomatoes, drained
2 tablespoons chopped pitted ripe olives
1 teaspoon minced garlic
2 tablespoons chopped fresh parsley

1. Preheat oven to 400°F. Spray 13×9-inch baking dish with nonstick olive oil cooking spray. Arrange cod fillets in prepared dish; season to taste with salt and pepper, if desired.

2. Combine tomatoes, olives and garlic in medium bowl. Spoon over fish.

3. Bake 20 minutes or until fish flakes easily when tested with fork. Sprinkle with parsley. **Makes 4 servings**

Serving Suggestion: For a great side, spread softened butter on French bread; sprinkle with paprika and oregano and broil until lightly toasted.

Prep and Cook Time: 25 minutes

Nutrients per Serving (¼ of total recipe [without bread side]):

Calories 121	Protein 21g
Fat 1g	Carbohydrate 5g
Calories from Fat 9%	Fiber 1g
Saturated Fat <1g	Sodium 574mg
Cholesterol 48mg	

Dietary Exchanges: 1 Vegetable, 2½ Lean Meat

Baked Cod with Tomatoes and Olives

Thai Salad Rolls with Spicy Sweet & Sour Sauce

Spicy Sweet & Sour Sauce (recipe follows)
3 ounces rice stick noodles
¼ pound raw medium or large shrimp, peeled and deveined
1 large bunch green leaf lettuce or Boston bibb lettuce
1 medium cucumber, peeled, seeded and cut into matchstick-size pieces
½ cup chopped fresh cilantro leaves
½ cup chopped fresh mint leaves

1. Prepare Spicy Sweet & Sour Sauce; set aside. Soak noodles in hot water 10 minutes. Rinse under cold running water to cool; drain.

2. Meanwhile, fill medium saucepan with water. Bring to a boil. Add shrimp; return to a boil. Cook 3 to 5 minutes or until shrimp turn pink; drain. Rinse under cold running water to cool. Split each shrimp lengthwise in half.

3. Select the 12 best and largest leaves of lettuce. Rinse under cold running water; pat dry.

4. To assemble rolls, place lettuce leaf, dark glossy side down, on work surface. Arrange shrimp, noodles, cucumber, cilantro and mint lengthwise along center rib of leaf. Roll up leaves as tightly as possible, taking care not to split leaves; secure with toothpicks. Remove toothpicks before eating. Serve rolls with Spicy Sweet & Sour Sauce. Garnish, if desired. **Makes 6 servings**

Spicy Sweet & Sour Sauce

1 green onion with top
2 tablespoons rice vinegar
1 tablespoon cornstarch
¾ cup water
¼ cup packed brown sugar
½ teaspoon red pepper flakes
2 tablespoons finely grated turnip

1. Finely chop white part of green onion; cut green portion into thin, 1-inch strips. Reserve green strips for garnish.

2. Combine vinegar and cornstarch in small bowl; mix well. Set aside.

3. Combine water, brown sugar, red pepper flakes and chopped green onion in small saucepan; bring to a boil.

4. Stir in cornstarch mixture. Return to a boil; cook 1 minute or until sauce is clear and thickened. Cool. Sprinkle with turnip and reserved green onion strips just before serving.   **Makes 6 servings**

Nutrients per Serving (2 Rolls with about 2 tablespoons Sauce):

Calories 122	Protein 5g
Fat <1g	Carbohydrate 23g
Calories from Fat 5%	Fiber <1g
Saturated Fat <1g	Sodium 54mg
Cholesterol 37mg	

Dietary Exchanges: 1½ Starch, ½ Lean Meat

Grilled Tuna with Salsa Salad

1 bag (16 ounces) BIRDS EYE® frozen Farm Fresh Mixtures
   Broccoli, Corn & Red Peppers
6 to 8 green onions, sliced
1 to 2 jalapeño peppers, finely chopped
1 can (14½ ounces) diced tomatoes with garlic and onion*
1 tablespoon, or to taste, lime juice or vinegar
4 tuna steaks, grilled as desired

Or substitute favorite seasoned diced tomatoes.

• In large saucepan, cook vegetables according to package directions; drain.

• In large bowl, combine vegetables, onions, peppers, tomatoes and lime juice. Let stand 15 minutes.

• Serve vegetable mixture over tuna.   **Makes 4 servings**

Prep Time: 5 minutes
Cook Time: 5 to 6 minutes

Nutrients per Serving (¼ of total recipe [with 3 ounces Grilled Tuna]):

Calories 232	Protein 30g
Fat 6g	Carbohydrate 17g
Calories from Fat 22%	Fiber 5g
Saturated Fat 1g	Sodium 716mg
Cholesterol 42mg	

Dietary Exchanges: 3 Vegetable, 3 Lean Meat

Caribbean Shrimp with Rice

1 package (12 ounces) frozen shrimp, thawed
½ cup fat-free reduced-sodium chicken broth
1 clove garlic, minced
1 teaspoon chili powder
½ teaspoon salt
½ teaspoon dried oregano leaves
1 cup frozen peas, thawed
½ cup diced tomatoes
2 cups cooked long-grain white rice

Slow Cooker Directions

1. Combine shrimp, broth, garlic, chili powder, salt and oregano in slow cooker. Cover; cook on LOW 2 hours.

2. Add peas and tomatoes. Cover; cook on LOW 5 minutes. Stir in rice. Cover; cook on LOW an additional 5 minutes. Garnish as desired.

Makes 4 servings

Nutrients per Serving (¼ of total recipe):

Calories 238	Protein 23g
Fat 2g	Carbohydrate 31g
Calories from Fat 9%	Fiber 3g
Saturated Fat <1g	Sodium 492mg
Cholesterol 132mg	

Dietary Exchanges: 2 Starch, 2½ Lean Meat

Caribbean Shrimp with Rice

Garlic Clams

2 pounds raw littleneck clams
2 teaspoons olive oil
2 tablespoons finely chopped onion
2 tablespoons chopped garlic
½ cup dry white wine
¼ cup chopped red bell pepper
2 tablespoons lemon juice
1 tablespoon chopped fresh parsley
Fresh parsley sprigs, for garnish (optional)

1. Discard any clams that remain open when tapped with fingers. To clean clams, scrub with stiff brush under cold running water. Soak clams in mixture of ½ cup salt to 1 gallon water 20 minutes. Drain water. Repeat 2 more times.

2. Heat oil in large saucepan over medium-high heat until hot. Add onion and garlic; cook and stir about 3 minutes or until garlic is tender but not brown.

3. Add clams, wine, bell pepper and lemon juice. Cover; simmer 3 to 10 minutes or until clams open. Transfer clams, as they open, to large bowl; cover. Discard any clams that do not open.

4. Increase heat to high. Add 1 tablespoon chopped parsley; boil until liquid reduces to ¼ to ⅓ cup. Pour over clams. Serve immediately. Garnish with fresh parsley sprigs, if desired.

Makes 4 servings

Nutrients per Serving (¼ of total recipe):

Calories 107	Protein 10g
Fat 3g	Carbohydrate 5g
Calories from Fat 25%	Fiber <1g
Saturated Fat <1g	Sodium 44mg
Cholesterol 25mg	

Dietary Exchanges: 1 Vegetable, 1 Lean Meat, ½ Fat

Garlic Clams

Tuna Noodle Casserole

6 ounces uncooked noodles (about 4 cups)
1 tablespoon margarine
8 ounces fresh mushrooms, sliced
1 small onion, chopped
1 cup fat-free reduced-sodium chicken broth
1 cup fat-free (skim) milk
¼ cup all-purpose flour
1 can (12 ounces) tuna packed in water, drained
1 cup frozen peas
1 jar (2 ounces) chopped pimiento, drained
½ teaspoon dried thyme leaves
¼ teaspoon salt
⅛ teaspoon black pepper

1. Preheat oven to 350°F. Cook noodles according to package directions, omitting salt. Drain; cover. Set aside.

2. Meanwhile, melt margarine in large nonstick skillet over medium-high heat. Add mushrooms and onion; cook and stir 5 minutes or until onion is tender.

3. Using wire whisk, blend chicken broth, milk and flour in small bowl. Stir into mushroom mixture in skillet; bring to a boil. Cook and stir about 2 minutes or until thickened. Reduce heat to medium. Stir in tuna, peas, pimiento, thyme, salt and pepper. Add noodles; mix thoroughly. (Casserole can be served at this point.)

4. Spray shallow 2-quart casserole with nonstick cooking spray. Spread noodle mixture evenly into prepared casserole: Bake 30 minutes or until bubbly and heated through. Let stand 5 minutes before serving. **Makes 6 servings**

Nutrients per Serving (1 cup Casserole [⅙ of total recipe]):

Calories 254	Protein 23g
Fat 3g	Carbohydrate 33g
Calories from Fat 11%	Fiber 2g
Saturated Fat 1g	Sodium 585mg
Cholesterol 18mg	

Dietary Exchanges: 2 Starch, 2 Lean Meat

Tuna Noodle Casserole

Grilled Fish with Orange-Chile Salsa

3 medium oranges, peeled and sectioned* (about 1¼ cups
  segments)
¼ cup finely diced green, red or yellow bell pepper
3 tablespoons chopped fresh cilantro, divided
3 tablespoons lime juice, divided
1 tablespoon honey
1 teaspoon minced, seeded serrano pepper *or* 1 tablespoon
  minced jalapeño pepper
1¼ pounds firm white fish fillets, such as orange roughy, lingcod,
  halibut or red snapper
  Lime slices
  Zucchini ribbons, cooked

*Canned mandarin orange segments can be substituted for fresh orange
segments, if desired.*

To prepare Orange-Chile Salsa, combine orange segments, bell
pepper, 2 tablespoons cilantro, 2 tablespoons lime juice, honey and
serrano pepper. Set aside.

Season fish fillets with remaining 1 tablespoon cilantro and
1 tablespoon lime juice. Lightly oil grid to prevent sticking. Grill fish
on covered grill over medium KINGSFORD® Briquets 5 minutes. Turn
and top with lime slices, if desired. Grill about 5 minutes until fish
flakes easily when tested with fork. Serve with Orange-Chile Salsa.
Garnish with zucchini ribbons. **Makes 4 servings**

Note: Allow about 10 minutes grilling time per inch thickness of fish
fillets.

Nutrients per Serving (¼ of total recipe):

Calories 154	Protein 21g
Fat 1g	Carbohydrate 14g
Calories from Fat 7%	Fiber <1g
Saturated Fat <1g	Sodium 88mg
Cholesterol 28mg	

Dietary Exchanges: 1 Fruit, 3 Lean Meat

Grilled Fish with Orange-Chile Salsa

Jamaican Shrimp & Pineapple Kabobs

½ cup prepared jerk sauce
¼ cup pineapple preserves
2 tablespoons minced fresh chives
1 pound raw large shrimp, peeled and deveined
½ medium pineapple, peeled, cored and cut into 1-inch cubes
2 large red, green or yellow bell peppers, cut into 1-inch
    squares

1. Prepare grill for direct grilling. Combine jerk sauce, preserves and chives in small bowl; mix well. Thread shrimp, pineapple and peppers onto 4 skewers; brush with jerk sauce mixture.

2. Grill kabobs over medium-hot coals 6 to 10 minutes or until shrimp turn pink and opaque, turning once. Serve with remaining jerk sauce mixture. **Makes 4 servings**

Tip: You can find pineapple already trimmed and cored in the produce section of your local supermarket.

Serving Suggestion: Serve kabobs with hot cooked rice.

Prep and Cook Time: 25 minutes

Nutrients per Serving (1 Kabob [without rice]):

Calories 226	Protein 20g
Fat 3g	Carbohydrate 31g
Calories from Fat 12%	Fiber 2g
Saturated Fat g	Sodium 262mg
Cholesterol 175mg	

Dietary Exchanges: 1½ Fruit, 1½ Vegetable, 2½ Lean Meat

Jamaican Shrimp & Pineapple Kabobs

chapter eight

Meatless

South-of-the-Border Lunch Express

½ cup chopped fresh tomato
¼ cup chunky salsa
¼ cup canned black beans, rinsed and drained
¼ cup frozen whole kernel corn, thawed
1 teaspoon chopped fresh cilantro
¼ teaspoon chopped garlic
   Dash ground red pepper
1 cup cooked brown rice
   Reduced-fat shredded Cheddar cheese (optional)

Microwave Directions

1. Combine tomato, salsa, beans, corn, cilantro, garlic and ground red pepper in 1-quart microwavable bowl. Cover with vented plastic wrap. Microwave at HIGH 1 to 1½ minutes or until heated through; stir.

2. Microwave rice in 1-quart microwavable dish at HIGH 1 to 1½ minutes or until heated through. Top with tomato mixture and cheese, if desired.   **Makes 1 serving**

Nutrients per Serving (total recipe [without cheese]):
Calories 345   Protein 14g
Fat 3g   Carbohydrate 74g
Calories from Fat 7%   Fiber 11g
Saturated Fat <1g   Sodium 610mg
Cholesterol 0mg

Dietary Exchanges: 4½ Starch, 1½ Vegetable, ½ Fat

South-of-the-Border Lunch Express

Cheese Ravioli with Pumpkin Sauce

Nonstick cooking spray
$\frac{1}{3}$ cup sliced green onions
1 to 2 cloves garlic, minced
$\frac{1}{2}$ teaspoon fennel seeds
1 cup evaporated skimmed milk
1 tablespoon all-purpose flour
$\frac{1}{4}$ teaspoon salt
$\frac{1}{8}$ teaspoon black pepper
$\frac{1}{2}$ cup solid-pack pumpkin
2 packages (9 ounces each) uncooked refrigerated low-fat
    cheese ravioli
2 tablespoons grated Parmesan cheese (optional)

1. Spray medium nonstick saucepan with cooking spray; heat over medium heat until hot. Add green onions, garlic and fennel seeds; cook and stir 3 minutes or until onions are tender.

2. Combine milk, flour, salt and pepper in small bowl until smooth; stir into saucepan. Bring to a boil over high heat; boil until thickened, stirring constantly. Stir in pumpkin. Reduce heat to low.

3. Meanwhile, cook pasta according to package directions, omitting salt. Drain. Divide ravioli evenly among 6 plates; top each with equal amount of pumpkin sauce. Sprinkle cheese evenly over top of each serving, if desired. Serve immediately. Garnish as desired.

Makes 6 servings

Nutrients per Serving ($\frac{1}{6}$ of total recipe [without cheese and garnish]):

Calories 270	Protein 18g
Fat 2g	Carbohydrate 45g
Calories from Fat 7%	Fiber 1g
Saturated Fat 1g	Sodium 556mg
Cholesterol 6mg	

Dietary Exchanges: 3 Starch, 1 Lean Meat

Cheese Ravioli with Pumpkin Sauce

Hot Three-Bean Casserole

2 tablespoons olive oil
1 cup coarsely chopped onion
1 cup chopped celery
2 cloves garlic, minced
1 can (15 ounces) chick-peas, rinsed and drained
1 can (15 ounces) kidney beans, rinsed and drained
1 cup coarsely chopped fresh tomato
1 can (8 ounces) tomato sauce
1 cup water
1 to 2 jalapeño peppers,* minced
1 tablespoon chili powder
2 teaspoons sugar
1½ teaspoons ground cumin
1 teaspoon salt
1 teaspoon dried oregano leaves
¼ teaspoon black pepper
2½ cups (10 ounces) frozen cut green beans
    Fresh oregano, for garnish (optional)

Jalapeño peppers can sting and irritate the skin. Wear rubber gloves when handling peppers and do not touch eyes. Wash hands after handling.

1. Heat olive oil in large skillet over medium heat until hot. Add onion, celery and garlic. Cook and stir 5 minutes or until onion is translucent.

2. Add remaining ingredients except green beans. Bring to a boil; reduce heat to low. Simmer, uncovered, 20 minutes. Add green beans. Simmer, uncovered, 10 minutes or until green beans are just tender. Garnish with fresh oregano, if desired. **Makes 6 servings**

Nutrients per Serving (1 cup Casserole):

Calories 236	Protein 12g
Fat 6g	Carbohydrate 40g
Calories from Fat 23%	Fiber 12g
Saturated Fat <1g	Sodium 1,042mg
Cholesterol 0mg	

Dietary Exchanges: 2 Starch, 2 Vegetable, ½ Lean Meat, ½ Fat

Hot Three-Bean Casserole

Saucy Broccoli and Spaghetti

3 ounces uncooked spaghetti
1 package (10 ounces) frozen chopped broccoli
½ cup thinly sliced leek, white part only
½ cup fat-free (skim) milk
2 teaspoons cornstarch
2 teaspoons chopped fresh oregano *or* ½ teaspoon dried
    oregano leaves, crushed
⅛ teaspoon hot pepper sauce
3 tablespoons reduced-fat cream cheese, softened
1 tablespoon grated Romano or Parmesan cheese
1 tablespoon chopped fresh parsley

1. Prepare spaghetti according to package directions, omitting salt; drain and keep warm. Meanwhile, cook broccoli and leek together according to package directions for broccoli, omitting salt. Drain; reserve ¼ cup liquid. Add additional water, if needed, to make ¼ cup.

2. Combine milk, cornstarch, oregano and pepper sauce in medium saucepan. Stir in reserved ¼ cup liquid. Cook and stir over medium heat until mixture boils and thickens. Stir in cream cheese. Cook and stir until cheese melts. Stir in vegetables; heat through.

3. Serve vegetable mixture over pasta. Sprinkle with Romano cheese and parsley. Garnish as desired.   **Makes 4 servings**

Nutrients per Serving (¼ of total recipe [without garnish]):

Calories 162	Protein 8g
Fat 3g	Carbohydrate 26g
Calories from Fat 16%	Fiber 3g
Saturated Fat 2g	Sodium 133mg
Cholesterol 9mg	

Dietary Exchanges: 1½ Starch, 1 Vegetable, ½ Fat

Saucy Broccoli and Spaghetti

Picante Pintos and Rice

2 cups uncooked dried pinto beans
Water
1 can (14½ ounces) no-salt-added stewed tomatoes
1 cup coarsely chopped onion
¾ cup coarsely chopped green bell pepper
¼ cup sliced celery
4 cloves garlic, minced
½ small jalapeño pepper,* seeded and chopped
2 teaspoons dried oregano leaves
2 teaspoons chili powder
½ teaspoon ground red pepper
2 cups chopped raw kale
3 cups hot cooked rice

Jalapeño peppers can sting and irritate the skin. Wear rubber gloves when handling peppers and do not touch eyes. Wash hands after handling.

1. Place beans in large saucepan; add water to cover beans by 2 inches. Bring to a boil over high heat; boil 2 minutes. Remove pan from heat; let stand, covered, 1 hour. Drain beans; discard water. Return beans to saucepan.

2. Add 2 cups water, tomatoes, onion, bell pepper, celery, garlic, jalapeño pepper, oregano, chili powder and ground red pepper to saucepan; bring to a boil over high heat. Reduce heat to low. Simmer, covered, about 1½ hours or until beans are tender, stirring occasionally.

3. Gently stir kale into bean mixture. Simmer, uncovered, 30 minutes. (Beans will be very tender and mixture will be consistency of thick sauce.) Serve over rice.   **Makes 8 servings**

Nutrients per Serving (⅛ of bean mixture with about ⅓ cup rice):

Calories 270	Protein 13g
Fat 1g	Carbohydrate 53g
Calories from Fat 4%	Fiber 13g
Saturated Fat <1g	Sodium 35mg
Cholesterol 0mg	

Dietary Exchanges: 3 Starch, 1½ Vegetable

Spinach Cheese Roulade

4 teaspoons FLEISCHMANN'S® Original Margarine, divided
2 tablespoons all-purpose flour
1 cup skim milk
2 cups EGG BEATERS® Healthy Real Egg Product
1 medium onion, chopped
1 (10-ounce) package fresh spinach, coarsely chopped
½ cup low-fat cottage cheese (1% milkfat)
1 (8-ounce) can no-salt-added tomato sauce
½ teaspoon dried basil leaves
½ teaspoon garlic powder

In small saucepan, over medium heat, melt 3 teaspoons margarine; blend in flour. Cook, stirring until smooth and bubbly; remove from heat. Gradually blend in milk; return to heat. Heat to a boil, stirring constantly until thickened; cool slightly. Stir in Egg Beaters®. Spread mixture in bottom of 15½×10½×1-inch baking pan that has been greased, lined with foil and greased again. Bake at 350°F for 20 minutes or until set.

In medium skillet, sauté onion in remaining margarine until tender. Add spinach and cook until wilted, about 3 minutes; stir in cottage cheese. Keep warm.

Invert egg mixture onto large piece of foil. Spread with spinach mixture; roll up from short end. In small saucepan, combine tomato sauce, basil and garlic; heat until warm. To serve, slice roll into 8 pieces; top with warm sauce. **Makes 8 servings**

Prep Time: 30 minutes
Cook Time: 25 minutes

Nutrients per Serving (1 slice Roulade with about 2 tablespoons sauce [⅛ of total recipe]):

Calories 92	Protein 10g
Fat 2g	Carbohydrate 7g
Calories from Fat 22%	Fiber 3g
Saturated Fat 1g	Sodium 233mg
Cholesterol 1mg	

Dietary Exchanges: 1½ Vegetable, 1 Lean Meat

Mediterranean Stew

1 medium butternut or acorn squash, peeled and cut into
    1-inch cubes
2 cups unpeeled eggplant, cut into 1-inch cubes
2 cups sliced zucchini
1 can (15½ ounces) chick-peas, rinsed and drained
1 package (10 ounces) frozen cut okra
1 can (8 ounces) tomato sauce
1 cup chopped onion
1 medium tomato, chopped
1 medium carrot, thinly sliced
½ cup reduced-sodium vegetable broth
⅓ cup raisins
1 clove garlic, minced
½ teaspoon ground cumin
½ teaspoon ground turmeric
¼ to ½ teaspoon ground red pepper
¼ teaspoon ground cinnamon
¼ teaspoon paprika
6 to 8 cups hot cooked couscous or rice
    Fresh parsley (optional)

Slow Cooker Directions
Combine all ingredients except couscous and parsley in slow cooker;
mix well. Cover; cook on LOW 8 to 10 hours or until vegetables are
crisp-tender. Serve over couscous. Garnish with parsley, if desired.

Makes 6 servings

Nutrients per Serving (⅙ of total recipe):

Calories 394	Protein 14g
Fat 2g	Carbohydrate 83g
Calories from Fat 4%	Fiber 12g
Saturated Fat <1g	Sodium 484mg
Cholesterol 0mg	

Dietary Exchanges: 4 Starch, 4 Vegetable

Mediterranean Stew

Vegetable Stir-Fry in Spicy Black Bean Sauce

1 teaspoon vegetable oil
1 medium onion, chopped
1 medium green bell pepper, cut into strips
3 carrots, cut into julienne strips (matchstick size)
3 cups shredded cabbage (green, red or napa)
1 cup tofu, crumbled
4 cups cooked rice, kept warm
   Fresh chives and radishes (optional)
Black Bean Sauce
   1 cup GUILTLESS GOURMET® Spicy Black Bean Dip
   2 teaspoons water
   $1/4$ cup low-sodium soy sauce
   $1/4$ cup cooking sherry
   1 tablespoon minced peeled fresh ginger
   1 clove garlic, minced

Heat oil in wok or large skillet over medium-high heat until hot. Add onion, pepper, carrots, cabbage and tofu; stir-fry until crisp-tender.

To prepare Black Bean Sauce, combine bean dip and water in small bowl; mix well. Stir in remaining Black Bean Sauce ingredients; pour over stir-fried vegetables. Stir-fry over high heat 2 minutes more. Reduce heat to low; cook 2 to 4 minutes more or until heated through, stirring often. Serve over hot rice. Garnish with chives and radishes, if desired.   **Makes 6 servings**

Nutrients per Serving ($1/6$ of total recipe [without garnish]):

Calories 267	Protein 9g
Fat 3g	Carbohydrate 46g
Calories from Fat 11%	Fiber 5g
Saturated Fat <1g	Sodium 566mg
Cholesterol 0mg	

Dietary Exchanges: 2 Starch, 3 Vegetable, 1 Lean Meat

Vegetable Stir-Fry in Spicy Black Bean Sauce

Vegetable Strata

2 slices white bread, cubed
¼ cup shredded reduced-fat Swiss cheese
½ cup sliced carrots
½ cup sliced mushrooms
¼ cup chopped onion
1 clove garlic, crushed
1 teaspoon FLEISCHMANN'S® Original Margarine
½ cup chopped tomato
½ cup snow peas
1 cup EGG BEATERS® Healthy Real Egg Product
¾ cup skim milk

Place bread cubes evenly on bottom of greased 1½-quart casserole dish. Sprinkle with cheese; set aside.

In medium nonstick skillet, over medium heat, sauté carrots, mushrooms, onion and garlic in margarine until tender. Stir in tomato and snow peas; cook 1 to 2 minutes more. Spoon over cheese. In small bowl, combine Egg Beaters® and milk; pour over vegetable mixture. Bake at 375°F for 45 to 50 minutes or until knife inserted into center comes out clean. Let stand 10 minutes before serving.

Makes 6 servings

Prep Time: 15 minutes
Cook Time: 55 minutes

Nutrients per Serving (⅙ of total recipe):

Calories 83	Protein 8g
Fat 1g	Carbohydrate 10g
Calories from Fat 13%	Fiber 1g
Saturated Fat <1g	Sodium 161mg
Cholesterol 3mg	

Dietary Exchanges: 2 Vegetable, ½ Lean Meat

Vegetable Strata

Tofu Stir-Fry

2 cups uncooked instant rice
2 teaspoons vegetable oil
2 cups broccoli florets
1 large carrot, sliced
½ green bell pepper, sliced
¼ cup chopped onion
½ cup teriyaki sauce
½ cup orange juice
1 tablespoon cornstarch
1 teaspoon minced garlic
½ teaspoon ground ginger
¼ to ½ teaspoon hot pepper sauce
1 package (10½ ounces) reduced-fat firm tofu, drained and cubed
Red bell pepper strips, for garnish (optional)

1. Cook rice according to package directions.

2. Meanwhile, heat oil in large skillet. Add broccoli, carrot, bell pepper and onion; cook and stir 3 minutes.

3. Combine teriyaki sauce, orange juice, cornstarch, garlic, ginger and pepper sauce in small bowl; mix well. Pour sauce over vegetables in skillet. Bring to a boil; cook and stir 1 minute.

4. Add tofu to skillet; stir gently to coat with sauce. Serve over rice. Garnish with red bell pepper strips, if desired.   **Makes 4 servings**

Prep and Cook Time: 18 minutes

Nutrients per Serving (¼ of total recipe):

Calories 318	Protein 13g
Fat 3g	Carbohydrate 59g
Calories from Fat 10%	Fiber 3g
Saturated Fat <1g	Sodium 844mg
Cholesterol 0mg	

Dietary Exchanges: 3 Starch, 3 Vegetable, ½ Fat

Tofu Stir-Fry

Chile, Egg & Cheese Casserole

1 tablespoon WESSON® Vegetable Oil, divided
½ cup *each:* chopped green bell pepper, red bell pepper and
  yellow bell pepper
1 cup chopped onion
2 jalapeño peppers, seeded and minced
3 containers (8 ounces each) fat free egg substitute (or
  12 eggs)
1 teaspoon salt
10 corn tortillas, torn into bits
1 can (14.5 ounces) HUNT'S® Diced Tomatoes in Juice
1½ cups low fat shredded Cheddar cheese, divided
  PAM® No-Stick Cooking Spray
1 tablespoon chopped fresh cilantro

1. Preheat oven to 400°F.

2. In large skillet, heat ½ *tablespoon* of Wesson® Oil over medium-high heat. Sauté bell peppers, onion and jalapeños until tender, about 5 minutes.

3. Meanwhile, in large mixing bowl, combine egg substitute and salt; stir in tortillas. When vegetables are cooked, stir into egg mixture.

4. Pour *remaining* oil into skillet; heat over medium heat. Add egg mixture and cook about 2 minutes, or until eggs are halfway cooked; remove from heat. Stir in Hunt's® Diced Tomatoes in Juice and ¾ *cup* cheese.

5. Transfer egg mixture to 13×9×2-inch baking dish, lightly sprayed with PAM® Cooking Spray. Top with *remaining* cheese.

6. Bake, uncovered, about 25 minutes, or until lightly browned. Sprinkle with cilantro.   **Makes 10 (8-ounce) servings**

Nutrients per Serving (1 [8-ounce] Casserole wedge [¹⁄₁₀ of total recipe] made with egg substitute):

Calories 158	Protein 14g
Fat 3g	Carbohydrate 18g
Calories from Fat 20%	Fiber 2g
Saturated Fat 1g	Sodium 640mg
Cholesterol 4mg	

Dietary Exchanges: 1 Starch, ½ Vegetable, 1½ Lean Meat

Black Bean Tostadas

1 cup canned black beans, rinsed, drained and mashed
2 teaspoons chili powder
  Nonstick cooking spray
4 (8-inch) corn tortillas
1 cup torn washed romaine lettuce leaves
1 cup chopped seeded fresh tomato
½ cup chopped onion
½ cup plain nonfat yogurt
2 jalapeño peppers,* seeded and finely chopped
  Fresh cilantro, tomato and green bell pepper slices, for
    garnish (optional)

Jalapeño peppers can sting and irritate the skin. Wear rubber gloves when handling peppers and do not touch eyes. Wash hands after handling.

1. Combine beans and chili powder in small saucepan. Cook over medium heat 5 minutes or until heated through, stirring occasionally.

2. Spray large nonstick skillet with cooking spray. Heat over medium heat until hot. Sprinkle tortillas with water; place in skillet, one at a time. Cook 20 to 30 seconds or until hot and pliable, turning once during cooking.

3. Spread bean mixture evenly over tortillas; layer with lettuce, tomato, onion, yogurt and peppers. Garnish with cilantro, sliced tomatoes and peppers, if desired. Serve immediately.

Makes 4 servings

Nutrients per Serving (1 Tostada):

Calories 146	Protein 9g
Fat 2g	Carbohydrate 29g
Calories from Fat 9%	Fiber 5g
Saturated Fat <1g	Sodium 466mg
Cholesterol 1mg	

Dietary Exchanges: 1½ Starch, 1½ Vegetable

chapter nine

Sides

Ratatouille

$\frac{1}{2}$ pound eggplant, peeled and cut into $\frac{1}{2}$-inch cubes
1 small onion, sliced and separated into rings
1 small zucchini, thinly sliced
$\frac{1}{2}$ medium green bell pepper, chopped
1 tomato, cut into wedges
1 tablespoon grated Parmesan cheese
1 rib celery, chopped
$\frac{1}{4}$ teaspoon salt (optional)
$\frac{1}{4}$ teaspoon dried chervil leaves
$\frac{1}{4}$ teaspoon dried oregano leaves
$\frac{1}{8}$ teaspoon dried minced garlic
$\frac{1}{8}$ teaspoon dried thyme leaves
Dash ground pepper

Microwave Directions
Combine all ingredients in 2-quart microwavable casserole; cover.
Microwave at HIGH 7 to 10 minutes or until eggplant is translucent,
stirring every 3 minutes. **Makes 6 servings**

Nutrients per Serving ($\frac{1}{6}$ of total recipe):

Calories 29 Protein 1g
Fat 1g Carbohydrate 6g
Calories from Fat 15% Fiber 2g
Saturated Fat <1g Sodium 29mg
Cholesterol 1mg

Dietary Exchanges: 1 Vegetable

Ratatouille

Polenta Triangles

¹⁄₂ cup yellow corn grits

1¹⁄₂ cups fat-free reduced-sodium chicken broth, divided

2 cloves garlic, minced

¹⁄₂ cup (2 ounces) crumbled feta cheese

1 roasted red bell pepper,* peeled and finely chopped

To roast bell pepper, place pepper on foil-lined broiler pan; broil 15 minutes or until blackened on all sides, turning every 5 minutes. Place pepper in paper bag; close bag and let stand 15 minutes before peeling.

1. Combine grits and ¹⁄₂ cup chicken broth in small bowl; mix well. Set aside. Pour remaining 1 cup broth into large heavy saucepan; bring to a boil. Add garlic and moistened grits; mix well and return to a boil. Reduce heat to low. Cover; cook 20 minutes. Remove from heat; add feta cheese. Stir until cheese is completely melted. Add roasted bell pepper; mix well.

2. Spray 8-inch square pan with nonstick cooking spray. Spoon grits mixture into prepared pan. Press grits evenly into pan with wet fingertips. Refrigerate until cold.

3. Spray grid with nonstick cooking spray. Prepare grill for direct cooking. Turn polenta out onto cutting board and cut into 2-inch squares. Cut each square diagonally into 2 triangles.

4. Place polenta triangles on grid. Grill over medium-high heat 1 minute or until bottoms are lightly browned. Turn over; grill until browned and crisp. Serve warm or at room temperature.

Makes 8 servings

Nutrients per Serving (1 Triangle):

Calories 62	Protein 3g
Fat 2g	Carbohydrate 9g
Calories from Fat 26%	Fiber <1g
Saturated Fat 1g	Sodium 142mg
Cholesterol 6mg	

Dietary Exchanges: 1 Starch

Polenta Triangles

Oven-Roasted Peppers and Onions

Nonstick olive oil cooking spray
2 medium green bell peppers
2 medium red bell peppers
2 medium yellow bell peppers
4 small onions
1 teaspoon dried Italian seasoning
$\frac{1}{2}$ teaspoon dried basil leaves
$\frac{1}{4}$ teaspoon ground cumin

1. Preheat oven to 375°F. Spray 15×10-inch jelly-roll pan with cooking spray. Cut bell peppers into 1½-inch pieces. Cut onions into quarters. Place vegetables on prepared pan; spray with cooking spray. Bake 20 minutes; stir. Sprinkle with Italian seasoning, basil and cumin.

2. *Increase oven temperature to 425°F.* Bake 20 minutes or until edges are darkened and vegetables are crisp-tender.

Makes 6 servings

Nutrients per Serving (⅙ of total recipe):

Calories 84

Protein 3g

Fat 1g

Carbohydrate 20g

Calories from Fat 6%

Fiber 4g

Saturated Fat <1g

Sodium 4mg

Cholesterol 0mg

Dietary Exchanges: 3½ Vegetable

Oven-Roasted Peppers and Onions

Apple Stuffing

1 cup finely chopped onion
½ cup finely chopped celery
½ cup finely chopped unpeeled apple
1½ cups MOTT'S® Natural Apple Sauce
1 (8-ounce) package stuffing mix (original or cornbread)
1 cup low-fat reduced-sodium chicken broth
1½ teaspoons dried thyme leaves
1 teaspoon ground sage
½ teaspoon salt
½ teaspoon black pepper

1. Preheat oven to 350°F. Spray medium nonstick skillet with nonstick cooking spray. Heat over medium heat until hot. Add onion and celery; cook and stir about 5 minutes or until transparent. Add apple; cook and stir about 3 minutes or until golden. Transfer to large bowl. Stir in apple sauce, stuffing mix, broth, thyme, sage, salt and black pepper.

2. Loosely stuff chicken or turkey just before roasting or place stuffing in greased 8-inch square pan. Cover pan; bake 20 to 25 minutes or until hot. Refrigerate leftovers. **Makes 8 servings**

Tip: Cooked stuffing can also be used to fill centers of cooked acorn squash.

Nutrients per Serving (⅛ of total recipe [without chicken, turkey or squash]):

Calories 150	Protein 4g
Fat 2g	Carbohydrate 31g
Calories from Fat 8%	Fiber 2g
Saturated Fat <1g	Sodium 620mg
Cholesterol 0mg	

Dietary Exchanges: 1 Starch, 1 Fruit

Apple Stuffing

Asparagus Spears with Sun-Dried Tomatoes

½ cup sun-dried tomatoes (not packed in oil)
1 cup boiling water
1 clove garlic, minced
2 tablespoons balsamic vinegar
1 teaspoon sugar
¼ teaspoon dried oregano leaves
¼ teaspoon dried basil leaves
⅛ teaspoon black pepper
½ cup water
1 pound asparagus, trimmed

1. To reconstitute sun-dried tomatoes, place in small bowl and cover with 1 cup boiling water; let stand 30 minutes. Drain; coarsely chop. Process tomatoes and garlic in blender or food processor until smooth. Add vinegar, sugar, oregano, basil and pepper; blend well. Set aside.

2. Bring ½ cup water to a boil in large skillet over high heat. Add asparagus; return to a boil. Reduce heat to medium-low. Simmer, covered, about 5 minutes or until asparagus is crisp-tender. Drain. Serve hot or cold with tomato mixture.   **Makes 4 servings**

Nutrients per Serving (¼ of total recipe):

Calories 49	Protein 3g
Fat 1g	Carbohydrate 8g
Calories from Fat 13%	Fiber 1g
Saturated Fat <1g	Sodium 20mg
Cholesterol 0mg	

Dietary Exchanges: 2 Vegetable

Moroccan Couscous

1 cup low-sodium chicken broth
½ teaspoon ground cinnamon
⅛ teaspoon ground nutmeg
⅔ cup uncooked couscous
⅔ cup DOLE® Pitted Dates or Pitted Prunes, chopped
½ cup chopped green onions
⅓ cup DOLE® Golden or Seedless Raisins
3 tablespoons sliced almonds, toasted

• Combine broth, cinnamon and nutmeg in medium saucepan. Bring to boil.

• Stir in couscous, dates, green onions and raisins. Remove from heat; cover. Let stand 5 minutes.

• Stir couscous mixture with fork; spoon into serving dish. Sprinkle with almonds. **Makes 6 servings**

Prep Time: 5 minutes
Cook Time: 10 minutes

Nutrients per Serving (⅙ of total recipe):

Calories 195	Protein 4g
Fat 2g	Carbohydrate 39g
Calories from Fat 11%	Fiber 3g
Saturated Fat <1g	Sodium 11mg
Cholesterol 0mg	

Dietary Exchanges: 1½ Starch, 1 Fruit, ½ Fat

Grilled Vegetables

$\frac{1}{4}$ cup assorted minced fresh herbs (such as parsley, thyme, rosemary, oregano or basil)

1 small eggplant (about $\frac{3}{4}$ pound), cut into $\frac{1}{4}$-inch-thick slices

$\frac{1}{2}$ teaspoon salt

1 *each* red, green and yellow bell pepper, quartered and seeded

2 zucchini, cut lengthwise into $\frac{1}{4}$-inch-thick slices

1 fennel bulb, cut lengthwise into $\frac{1}{4}$-inch-thick slices

Nonstick cooking spray

1. Combine herbs in small bowl; let stand 3 hours or overnight.

2. Place eggplant in large colander over bowl; sprinkle with salt. Drain 1 hour.

3. Prepare grill for direct grilling. Spray vegetables with cooking spray and sprinkle with herb mixture. Grill 10 to 15 minutes or until fork-tender and lightly browned on both sides.*   **Makes 6 servings**

*Cooking times vary depending on type of vegetable. Remove vegetables as they are done, to avoid overcooking.

Variation: Cut vegetables into 1-inch cubes and thread onto skewers. Spray with cooking spray and sprinkle with herb mixture. Grill as directed above.

Nutrients per Serving ($\frac{1}{6}$ of total recipe):

Calories 34	Protein 1g
Fat <1g	Carbohydrate 8g
Calories from Fat 6%	Fiber 2g
Saturated Fat <1g	Sodium 190mg
Cholesterol 0mg	

Dietary Exchanges: $1\frac{1}{2}$ Vegetable

Grilled Vegetables

Apricot-Glazed Beets

1 large bunch fresh beets *or* 1 pound loose beets
1 cup apricot nectar
1 tablespoon cornstarch
2 tablespoons cider vinegar or red wine vinegar
8 dried apricot halves, cut into strips
¼ teaspoon salt
   Additional apricot halves (optional)

1. Cut tops off beets, leaving at least 1 inch of stems (do not trim root ends). Scrub beets under running water with soft vegetable brush, being careful not to break skins. Place beets in medium saucepan; cover with water. Bring to a boil over high heat. Reduce heat; cover and simmer about 20 minutes or until just barely firm when pierced with fork and skins rub off easily. Transfer to plate; cool. Rinse pan.

2. Combine apricot nectar and cornstarch in same saucepan; stir in vinegar. Add apricot strips and salt. Cook over medium heat until mixture thickens.

3. Cut roots and stems from beets on plate.* Peel, halve and cut beets into ¼-inch-thick slices. Add beet slices to apricot mixture; toss gently to coat. Transfer to warm serving dish. Garnish as desired. Serve immediately with apricot halves, if desired.

Makes 4 servings

Do not cut beets on cutting board; the juice will stain the board.

Nutrients per Serving (¼ of total recipe [without additional apricots]):
Calories 109   Protein 2g
Fat <1g   Carbohydrate 27g
Calories from Fat 2%   Fiber 4g
Saturated Fat 0g   Sodium 232mg
Cholesterol 0mg

Dietary Exchanges: 1 Fruit, 2 Vegetable

Apricot-Glazed Beets

Southern Greens and Pasta

2 teaspoons olive oil

1 cup chopped green bell pepper

½ cup chopped onion

½ cup peeled and chopped jicama

⅓ cup chopped celery

1 clove garlic, minced

1 can (14½ ounces) fat-free reduced-sodium chicken broth

2 tablespoons tomato paste

1 teaspoon dried oregano leaves

¼ teaspoon black pepper

1 package (10 ounces) frozen black-eyed peas

4 ounces uncooked radiatore or other medium pasta

1 head chicory, mustard greens or kale, washed, ribs removed, and thinly sliced

2 to 3 drops hot pepper sauce

1. Heat oil in large saucepan. Add bell pepper, onion, jicama, celery and garlic. Cook over medium heat 3 minutes. Stir in chicken broth, tomato paste, oregano and black pepper; bring to a boil. Stir in black-eyed peas. Cover; simmer over low heat 20 minutes or until peas are tender.

2. Cook pasta according to package directions, omitting salt. Drain and set aside.

3. Add chicory to saucepan. Cover; cook over low heat until wilted, about 3 minutes. Stir in pasta. Cook until heated through. Season to taste with red pepper sauce. Garnish as desired.

Makes 12 servings

Nutrients per Serving (½ cup [without garnish]):

Calories 88	Protein 4g
Fat 1g	Carbohydrate 15g
Calories from Fat 13%	Fiber 3g
Saturated Fat <1g	Sodium 39mg
Cholesterol 0mg	

Dietary Exchanges: 1 Starch, ½ Vegetable

Southern Greens and Pasta

Sweet and Russet Potato Latkes

2 cups shredded russet potatoes
1 cup shredded sweet potato
1 cup shredded apple
¾ cup cholesterol-free egg substitute
⅓ cup all-purpose flour
1 teaspoon sugar
¼ teaspoon baking powder
¼ teaspoon salt
⅛ teaspoon ground nutmeg
   Nonstick cooking spray
1 cup unsweetened cinnamon applesauce

1. Preheat oven to 250°F. Combine potatoes and apple in medium bowl. Combine egg substitute, flour, sugar, baking powder, salt and nutmeg in small bowl; add to potato mixture.

2. Spray large nonstick skillet with cooking spray; heat over medium-low heat until hot. Spoon 1 rounded tablespoonful potato mixture into skillet; flatten to form pancake about ¼ inch thick and 3 inches in diameter.* Cook 3 minutes or until browned. Turn over; cook 3 minutes or until browned. Repeat with remaining batter. Keep cooked latkes warm in oven.

3. Top each latke with 1 tablespoon applesauce. Garnish, if desired.

Makes 8 servings

Three to four latkes can be cooked at one time.

Nutrients per Serving (2 Latkes with 2 tablespoons applesauce
[1 tablespoon per Latke] without garnish):

Calories 107	Protein 4g
Fat <1g	Carbohydrate 23g
Calories from Fat 2%	Fiber 2g
Saturated Fat <1g	Sodium 119mg
Cholesterol 0mg	

Dietary Exchanges: 1 Starch, ½ Fruit

Sweet and Russet Potato Latkes

Spicy Thai Rice

2 cups water
1 cup uncooked long grain white rice
1/4 cup chopped green onions
2 fresh red chiles, seeded and chopped
1 tablespoon snipped cilantro
1 tablespoon margarine
1 teaspoon minced fresh gingerroot
3/4 teaspoon salt
1/8 teaspoon ground turmeric
1 to 2 teaspoons lime juice
    Chopped roasted peanuts for garnish (optional)
    Red pepper flakes for garnish (optional)

Combine water, rice, onions, chiles, cilantro, margarine, gingerroot, salt and turmeric in 2- to 3-quart saucepan. Bring to a boil; stir once or twice. Reduce heat; cover and simmer 15 minutes or until rice is tender and liquid is absorbed. Stir in lime juice; fluff with fork. Garnish with peanuts and pepper flakes.   **Makes 6 servings**

Favorite recipe from **USA Rice Federation**

Nutrients per Serving (1/6 of total recipe [without peanuts]):

Calories 138   Protein 3g
Fat 2g   Carbohydrate 26g
Calories from Fat 15%   Fiber 1g
Saturated Fat <1g   Sodium 317mg
Cholesterol 0mg

Dietary Exchanges: 1 1/2 Starch, 1/2 Fat

Brussels Sprouts with Lemon-Dill Glaze

1 pound brussels sprouts*
2 teaspoons cornstarch
½ teaspoon dried dill weed
½ cup fat-free reduced-sodium chicken broth
3 tablespoons lemon juice
½ teaspoon grated lemon peel

Or, substitute 1 package (10 ounces) frozen brussels sprouts. Cook according to package directions; drain.

1. Trim brussels sprouts. Cut an X in stem ends. Bring 1 cup water to a boil in large saucepan over high heat. Add brussels sprouts; return to a boil. Reduce heat to medium-low. Simmer, covered, 10 minutes or until just tender. Drain well; return to pan. Set aside.

2. Meanwhile, combine cornstarch and dill weed in small saucepan. Add chicken broth and lemon juice; blend until smooth. Stir in lemon peel. Cook and stir over medium heat 5 minutes or until mixture boils and thickens. Cook and stir 1 minute more.

3. Pour glaze over brussels sprouts; toss gently to coat. Serve hot.

Makes 4 servings

Nutrients per Serving (¼ of total recipe):

Calories 58	Protein 3g
Fat 1g	Carbohydrate 13g
Calories from Fat 9%	Fiber 5g
Saturated Fat <1g	Sodium 31mg
Cholesterol 0mg	

Dietary Exchanges: 2½ Vegetable

chapter ten

Breads

German Rye Beer Bread

1½-Pound Loaf

1¼ cups beer, at room temperature

2 tablespoons light molasses

1 tablespoon butter

1½ teaspoons salt

2 teaspoons caraway seeds

2½ cups bread flour

½ cup rye flour

1½ teaspoons rapid-rise yeast

2-Pound Loaf

1½ cups beer, at room temperature

3 tablespoons light molasses

1½ tablespoons butter

2 teaspoons salt

1 tablespoon caraway seeds

3¼ cups bread flour

¾ cup rye flour

2 teaspoons rapid-rise yeast

Bread Machine Directions

Place all ingredients in bread machine pan in order specified by owner's manual. Program basic cycle and desired crust setting; press start. Cool bread on wire rack.   **Makes 12 or 16 servings**

Nutrients per Serving (1 slice [¹⁄₁₂ of 1½-pound loaf or ¹⁄₁₆ of 2-pound loaf]):

Calories 144	Protein 4g
Fat 1g	Carbohydrate 28g
Calories from Fat 6%	Fiber 1g
Saturated Fat <1g	Sodium 279mg
Cholesterol 3mg	

Dietary Exchanges: 2 Starch

German Rye Beer Bread

Oatmeal-Raisin Bread

1½-Pound Loaf
   1¼ cups water
   2 tablespoons honey
   1 tablespoon margarine or butter, softened
   1½ teaspoons salt
   3 cups bread flour
   ¼ cup nonfat dry milk powder
   1½ teaspoons rapid-rise yeast
   ½ cup uncooked old-fashioned oats
   ½ cup raisins
2-Pound Loaf
   1½ cups water
   3 tablespoons honey
   2 tablespoons margarine or butter
   2 teaspoons salt
   4 cups bread flour
   ⅓ cup nonfat dry milk powder
   2 teaspoons rapid-rise yeast
   ¾ cup uncooked old-fashioned oats
   ¾ cup raisins

Bread Machine Directions

1. Measuring carefully, place all ingredients except oats and raisins in bread machine pan in order specified by owner's manual.

2. Program basic cycle and desired crust setting; press start. Add oats and raisins when bread machine signals, or at end of first kneading cycle. Remove baked bread from pan; cool on wire rack.

Makes 12 or 16 servings

Nutrients per Serving (1 slice [¹⁄₁₂ of 1½-pound loaf or ¹⁄₁₆ of 2-pound loaf]):

Calories 176	Protein 6g
Fat 2g	Carbohydrate 36g
Calories from Fat 10%	Fiber 1g
Saturated Fat <1g	Sodium 286mg
Cholesterol 3mg	

Dietary Exchanges: 2 Starch, ½ Fruit

Oatmeal–Raisin Bread

Low Fat Pumpkin Bread

1 cup Dried Plum Purée (recipe follows) or prepared dried
plum butter
1 cup packed brown sugar
1 cup granulated sugar
1 cup egg substitute
1 cup canned solid pack pumpkin
2²⁄₃ cups all-purpose flour
2 teaspoons baking powder
1 teaspoon baking soda
1 teaspoon ground cinnamon
¹⁄₂ teaspoon salt
¹⁄₂ teaspoon ground cloves
¹⁄₄ teaspoon ground ginger
¹⁄₄ teaspoon ground nutmeg

Preheat oven to 350°F. Coat two 8¹⁄₂×4¹⁄₂×2³⁄₄-inch loaf pans with
vegetable cooking spray. In mixer bowl, beat Dried Plum Purée with
sugars until well blended. Beat in egg substitute and pumpkin just
until blended. In medium bowl, combine flour, baking powder, baking
soda, cinnamon, salt, cloves, ginger and nutmeg; stir into Dried Plum
Purée mixture until well blended. Spoon batter into prepared pans,
dividing equally. Bake in center of oven 1 hour until pick inserted into
centers comes out clean. Cool in pans 10 minutes; remove from pans
to wire racks to cool completely. Serve with fat free cream cheese, if
desired. **Makes 2 loaves (16 slices per loaf)**

Dried Plum Purée: Combine 1¹⁄₃ cups (8 ounces) pitted dried
plums and 6 tablespoons hot water in container of food processor or
blender. Pulse on and off until dried plums are finely chopped and
smooth. Makes 1 cup.

Favorite recipe from **California Dried Plum Board**

Nutrients per Serving (1 slice [¹⁄₁₆ of 1 loaf]):

Calories 110	Protein 2g
Fat 1g	Carbohydrate 24g
Calories from Fat 1%	Fiber 1g
Saturated Fat <1g	Sodium 124mg
Cholesterol 0mg	

Dietary Exchanges: 1¹⁄₂ Starch

Low Fat Pumpkin Bread

Cranberry Scones

2½ cups all-purpose flour
½ cup packed brown sugar
1 tablespoon baking powder
1 teaspoon baking soda
¾ teaspoon salt
½ teaspoon ground cinnamon
¼ cup Dried Plum Purée (recipe follows) or prepared dried
plum butter
2 tablespoons cold margarine or butter
1 container (8 ounces) nonfat vanilla yogurt
¾ cup dried cranberries
1 egg white, lightly beaten
1 tablespoon granulated sugar

Preheat oven to 400°F. Coat baking sheet with vegetable cooking spray. In large bowl, combine flour, brown sugar, baking powder, baking soda, salt and cinnamon. Cut in Dried Plum Purée and margarine with pastry blender until mixture resembles coarse crumbs. Mix in yogurt just until blended. Stir in cranberries. On floured surface, roll or pat dough to ¾-inch thickness. Cut out with 2½- to 3-inch biscuit cutter, rerolling scraps as needed, but handling as little as possible. Arrange on prepared baking sheet, spacing 2 inches apart. Brush with egg white and sprinkle with granulated sugar. Bake in center of oven about 15 minutes until golden brown and springy to the touch. Serve warm or at room temperature.

Makes 12 scones

Dried Plum Purée: Combine 1⅓ cups (8 ounces) pitted dried plums and 6 tablespoons hot water in container of food processor or blender. Pulse on and off until dried plums are finely chopped and smooth. Store leftovers in a covered container in the refrigerator for up to two months. Makes 1 cup.

Favorite recipe from **California Dried Plum Board**

Nutrients per Serving (1 Scone):

Calories 198	Protein 4g
Fat 2g	Carbohydrate 41g
Calories from Fat 10%	Fiber 1g
Saturated Fat <1g	Sodium 415mg
Cholesterol 0mg	

Dietary Exchanges: 1½ Starch, 1 Fruit, ½ Fat

Cranberry Scones

French Twist Potato Bread

1 large COLORADO russet variety potato, peeled and cut up
5 ½ to 6 cups bread flour or all-purpose flour, divided
2 packages active dry yeast
1 teaspoon salt
1 egg white, lightly beaten
1 tablespoon water
1 teaspoon coarse-grained (Kosher) salt
1 teaspoon coarsely ground black pepper
Cornmeal

In saucepan combine potato and 1 cup water. Bring to a boil; reduce heat. Cover and simmer about 15 minutes or until potato is very tender. Mash potato in liquid. Add additional water to make 2 cups. Cool liquid mixture to 120° to 130°F.

In large mixing bowl combine 1 ½ cups flour, yeast, 1 teaspoon salt and warm potato mixture. Beat on low speed to mix well; then beat on high speed 3 minutes, scraping sides of bowl. Stir in as much of remaining flour as possible with spoon. Turn out onto floured surface and knead 8 to 10 minutes or until smooth and elastic. Place in greased bowl; let rise in warm place until doubled, about 1 hour.

Combine egg white and 1 tablespoon water; set aside. Punch down dough. Turn out onto floured surface; cut into 4 pieces and let rest 5 minutes. Roll each piece into 12- to 14-inch rope. Brush ropes lightly with some of egg white mixture; sprinkle lightly with coarse salt and pepper. For each loaf, twist 2 ropes together to form 1 loaf. Place loaves on greased and cornmeal-coated baking sheets. Let rise in warm place until nearly doubled, about 35 to 40 minutes. Bake in 375°F oven 35 to 40 minutes. Brush loaves with remaining egg white mixture about half way through baking time. Cool on wire rack.

Makes 2 loaves

Favorite recipe from **Colorado Potato Administrative Committee**

Nutrients per Serving (1 slice [$^1/_{12}$ of 1 loaf]):

Calories 121	Protein 4g
Fat 1g	Carbohydrate 24g
Calories from Fat 4%	Fiber 1g
Saturated Fat <1g	Sodium 197mg
Cholesterol 0mg	

Dietary Exchanges: 1 ½ Starch

Garlic and Herb Parmesan Buns

8 Buns
1¼ cups water
1 tablespoon sugar
1½ teaspoons salt
1 teaspoon garlic powder
2 teaspoons dried Italian seasoning
⅓ cup grated Parmesan cheese
3 cups bread flour
1 tablespoon quick-rise active dry yeast

12 Buns
1½ cups water
2 tablespoons sugar
2 teaspoons salt
1½ teaspoons garlic powder
1 tablespoon dried Italian seasoning
½ cup grated Parmesan cheese
4 cups bread flour
1 tablespoon quick-rise active dry yeast

Topping
1 to 2 tablespoons grated Parmesan cheese

Bread Machine Directions

1. Place all ingredients except topping in bread machine pan in order specified by owner's manual. Program dough cycle setting; press start.

2. Turn out dough onto surface lightly coated with nonstick cooking spray. Cut dough into 8 pieces for small batch or 12 pieces for large batch. Shape into smooth balls. Place on baking sheet lightly coated with cooking spray; flatten slightly. Let rise in warm place 45 minutes or until doubled. Preheat oven to 400°F. Brush buns with water; sprinkle tops with cheese. Bake 15 minutes or until lightly browned. Serve warm or transfer to wire racks to cool completely.

Makes 8 or 12 buns

Nutrients per Serving (1 Bun):
Calories 211
Fat 2g
Calories from Fat 9%
Saturated Fat <1g
Cholesterol 3mg
Protein 8g
Carbohydrate 41g
Fiber <1g
Sodium 479mg

Dietary Exchanges: 2½ Starch, ½ Fat

Miniature Fruit Muffins

1 cup whole wheat flour
¾ cup all-purpose flour
½ cup packed dark brown sugar
2 teaspoons baking powder
½ teaspoon baking soda
¼ teaspoon salt
1 cup buttermilk, divided
¾ cup frozen blueberries
1 small ripe banana, mashed
¼ teaspoon vanilla
⅓ cup unsweetened applesauce
2 tablespoons raisins
½ teaspoon ground cinnamon

1. Preheat oven to 400°F. Spray 36 miniature muffin cups with nonstick cooking spray; set aside.

2. Combine flours, sugar, baking powder, baking soda and salt in medium bowl. Place ⅔ cup dry ingredients in each of 3 medium bowls.

3. Add ⅓ cup buttermilk and blueberries to one bowl of flour mixture; stir just until blended. Spoon into 12 prepared muffin cups. Add ⅓ cup buttermilk, banana and vanilla to another bowl of flour mixture; stir just until blended. Spoon into 12 more prepared muffin cups. Add remaining ⅓ cup buttermilk, applesauce, raisins and cinnamon to remaining bowl of flour mixture; stir just until blended. Spoon into remaining 12 prepared muffin cups.

4. Bake 18 minutes or until lightly browned and toothpick inserted into centers comes out clean. Remove from pan. Cool 10 minutes on wire racks. Serve warm or cool completely.

Makes 3 dozen miniature muffins

Nutrients per Serving (3 Miniature Muffins, 1 of each flavor):

Calories 130	Protein 3g
Fat 1g	Carbohydrate 29g
Calories from Fat 4%	Fiber 2g
Saturated Fat <1g	Sodium 178mg
Cholesterol 1mg	

Dietary Exchanges: 1 Starch, 1 Fruit

Miniature Fruit Muffins

Pull–Apart Rye Rolls

¾ cup water
2 tablespoons margarine or butter, softened
2 tablespoons molasses
2¼ cups all-purpose flour, divided
½ cup rye flour
⅓ cup nonfat dry milk powder
1 package (¼ ounce) active dry yeast
1½ teaspoons salt
1½ teaspoons caraway seeds
    Melted margarine or vegetable oil

1. Heat water, margarine and molasses in small saucepan over low heat until temperature reaches 120° to 130°F. Combine 1¼ cups all-purpose flour, rye flour, milk powder, yeast, salt and caraway seeds in large bowl. Stir heated water mixture into flour mixture with wooden spoon to form soft but sticky dough. Gradually add more all-purpose flour until rough dough forms.

2. Turn out dough onto lightly floured surface. Knead 5 to 8 minutes or until smooth and elastic, gradually adding remaining flour to prevent sticking, if necessary. Cover with inverted bowl. Let rise 35 to 40 minutes or until dough has increased in bulk by one third. Punch down dough; divide in half. Roll each half into 12-inch log. Using sharp knife, cut each log evenly into 12 pieces; shape into tight balls. Arrange in greased 8- or 9-inch cake pan. Brush tops with melted margarine. Loosely cover with lightly greased sheet of plastic wrap. Let rise in warm place 45 minutes or until doubled in bulk.

3. Preheat oven to 375°F. Uncover rolls; bake 15 to 20 minutes or until golden brown. Cool in pan on wire rack 5 minutes. Remove from pan; cool completely on wire rack.   **Makes 2 dozen rolls**

Nutrients per Serving (1 Roll):

Calories 67	Protein 2g
Fat 1g	Carbohydrate 12g
Calories from Fat 13%	Fiber 1g
Saturated Fat <1g	Sodium 150mg
Cholesterol 3mg	

Dietary Exchanges: 1 Starch

Pull-Apart Rye Rolls

Apple Sauce Coffee Ring

BREAD

   1 package active dry yeast

   $1/3$ cup plus 1 teaspoon granulated sugar, divided

   $1/4$ cup warm water (105° to 115°F)

   $1/2$ cup skim milk

   $1/2$ cup MOTT'S® Natural Apple Sauce

   1 egg

   2 tablespoons margarine, melted and cooled

   1 teaspoon salt

   1 teaspoon grated lemon peel

   5 cups all-purpose flour

   1 teaspoon skim milk

FILLING

   $1 1/2$ cups MOTT'S® Chunky Apple Sauce

   $1/2$ cup raisins

   $1/3$ cup firmly packed light brown sugar

   1 teaspoon ground cinnamon

GLAZE

   1 cup powdered sugar

   2 tablespoons skim milk

   1 teaspoon vanilla extract

1. To prepare Bread, in large bowl, sprinkle yeast and 1 teaspoon granulated sugar over warm water; stir until yeast dissolves. Let stand 5 minutes or until mixture is bubbly. Stir in $1/2$ cup milk, $1/2$ cup natural apple sauce, remaining $1/3$ cup granulated sugar, egg, margarine, salt and lemon peel.

2. Stir in flour, 1 cup at a time, until soft dough forms. Turn out dough onto floured surface; flatten slightly. Knead 5 minutes or until smooth and elastic, adding any remaining flour to prevent sticking if necessary. Shape dough into ball; place in large bowl sprayed with nonstick cooking spray. Turn dough over so that top is greased. Cover with damp towel; let rise in warm place 1 hour or until doubled in bulk.

3. Punch down dough. Roll out dough on floured surface into 15-inch square. Spray baking sheet with nonstick cooking spray.

4. To prepare Filling, in small bowl, combine 1$\frac{1}{2}$ cups chunky apple sauce, raisins, brown sugar and cinnamon. Spread filling over dough, to within $\frac{1}{2}$ inch of edges. Roll up dough jelly-roll style. Moisten edge with water; pinch to seal seam. Moisten ends of dough with water; bring together to form ring. Pinch to seal seam. Place on prepared baking sheet. Make $\frac{1}{8}$-inch-deep cuts across width of dough at 2-inch intervals around ring.

5. Let dough rise in warm place, uncovered, 30 minutes.

6. Preheat oven to 350°F. Brush top of ring lightly with 1 teaspoon milk.

7. Bake 45 to 50 minutes or until lightly browned and ring sounds hollow when tapped. Remove from baking sheet; cool completely on wire rack.

8. To prepare Glaze, in small bowl, combine powdered sugar, 2 tablespoons milk and vanilla until smooth. Drizzle over top of ring. Cut into 24 slices. **Makes 24 servings**

Nutrients per Serving (1 slice [$\frac{1}{24}$ of total recipe]):

Calories 171	Protein 3g
Fat 1g	Carbohydrate 36g
Calories from Fat 8%	Fiber 1g
Saturated Fat <1g	Sodium 117mg
Cholesterol 9mg	

Dietary Exchanges: 1$\frac{1}{2}$ Starch, 1 Fruit

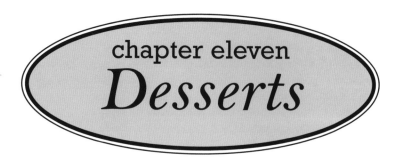

chapter eleven

Desserts

Spun Sugar Berries with Yogurt Crème

2 cups fresh raspberries*
1 container (8 ounces) lemon-flavored nonfat yogurt with
    aspartame sweetener
1 cup thawed frozen fat-free nondairy whipped topping
3 tablespoons sugar

Substitute your favorite fresh berries for the fresh raspberries, if desired.

1. Arrange berries in 4 glass dessert dishes.

2. Combine yogurt and whipped topping in medium bowl. (If not using immediately, cover and refrigerate.) Top berries with yogurt mixture.

3. To prepare spun sugar, pour sugar into heavy medium saucepan. Cook over medium-high heat until sugar melts, shaking pan occasionally. *Do not stir.* As sugar begins to melt, reduce heat to low and cook about 10 minutes or until sugar is completely melted and has turned light golden brown.

4. Remove from heat; let stand 1 minute. Coat metal fork with sugar mixture. Drizzle sugar over yogurt mixture with circular or back and forth motion. Ropes of spun sugar will harden quickly. Garnish as desired. Serve immediately. **Makes 4 servings**

Nutrients per Serving (1 dessert dish [¹/₄ of total recipe] made with fresh raspberries):

Calories 119	Protein 3g
Fat <1g	Carbohydrate 26g
Calories from Fat 2%	Fiber 4g
Saturated Fat <1g	Sodium 45mg
Cholesterol 0mg	

Dietary Exchanges: 2 Fruit

Spun Sugar Berries with Yogurt Crème

Scrumptious Apple Cake

3 egg whites
1½ cups sugar
1 cup unsweetened applesauce
1 teaspoon vanilla
2 cups all-purpose flour
2 teaspoons ground cinnamon
1 teaspoon baking soda
¼ teaspoon salt
4 cups cored peeled tart apple slices (McIntosh or Crispin)
Yogurt Glaze (recipe follows)

Preheat oven to 350°F. Beat egg whites until slightly foamy; add sugar, applesauce and vanilla. Combine flour, cinnamon, baking soda and salt in separate bowl; add to applesauce mixture. Spread apples in 9-inch round springform pan or 13×9-inch pan sprayed with nonstick cooking spray. Spread batter over apples. Bake 35 to 40 minutes or until wooden toothpick inserted into center comes out clean; cool on wire rack. Prepare Yogurt Glaze; spread over cooled cake.

Makes 15 to 20 servings

Yogurt Glaze: Combine 1½ cups plain or vanilla nonfat yogurt, 3 tablespoons brown sugar (or to taste) and 1 teaspoon vanilla or 1 teaspoon lemon juice. Stir together until smooth.

Favorite recipe from **New York Apple Association, Inc.**

Nutrients per Serving (1 Cake slice with about 1½ tablespoons Yogurt Glaze [¹⁄₁₅ of total recipe] without garnish):

Calories 189	Protein 4g
Fat <1g	Carbohydrate 43g
Calories from Fat 2%	Fiber 2g
Saturated Fat <1g	Sodium 155mg
Cholesterol <1mg	

Dietary Exchanges: 1 Starch, 2 Fruit

Scrumptious Apple Cake

Apricot Biscotti

3 cups all-purpose flour
1½ teaspoons baking soda
½ teaspoon salt
⅔ cup sugar
3 eggs
1 teaspoon vanilla
½ cup chopped dried apricots*
⅓ cup sliced almonds, chopped
1 tablespoon reduced-fat (2%) milk

Other chopped dried fruits, such as dried cherries, cranberries or blueberries, can be substituted.

1. Preheat oven to 350°F. Lightly coat cookie sheet with nonstick cooking spray; set aside.

2. Combine flour, baking soda and salt in medium bowl; set aside.

3. Beat sugar, eggs and vanilla in large bowl at medium speed of electric mixer until well blended. Add flour mixture; beat well.

4. Stir in apricots and almonds. Turn dough out onto lightly floured surface. Knead 4 to 6 times. Shape dough into 20-inch log; place on prepared cookie sheet. Brush dough with milk.

5. Bake 30 minutes or until firm. Remove from oven; cool 10 minutes. Diagonally cut into 30 slices. Place slices on cookie sheet. Bake 10 minutes; turn and bake additional 10 minutes. Cool completely on wire racks. Store in airtight container.   **Makes 2½ dozen biscotti**

Nutrients per Serving (1 Biscotti [made with dried apricots]):

Calories 86	Protein 2g
Fat 1g	Carbohydrate 16g
Calories from Fat 10%	Fiber 1g
Saturated Fat <1g	Sodium 108mg
Cholesterol 21mg	

Dietary Exchanges: 1 Starch

Apricot Biscotti

Luscious Lime Angel Food Cake Rolls

1 package (16 ounces) angel food cake mix
Green food coloring (optional)
2 containers (8 ounces each) lime-flavored nonfat yogurt with
aspartame sweetener
Lime slices, for garnish (optional)

1. Preheat oven to 350°F. Line two 17×11¼×1-inch jelly-roll pans with parchment or waxed paper; set aside.

2. Prepare angel food cake mix according to package directions. Divide batter evenly between prepared pans. Draw knife through batter to remove large air bubbles. Bake 12 minutes or until cakes are lightly browned and toothpick inserted into centers comes out clean.

3. Invert each cake onto separate clean towel. Starting at short end, roll up warm cake, jelly-roll fashion, with towel inside. Cool cakes completely.

4. Tint each container of yogurt green with food coloring, if desired; stir well. Unroll cakes; remove towels. Spread each cake with 1 container yogurt to within 1 inch of edges. Roll up cakes; place seam side down. Slice each cake roll into 8 pieces. Garnish with lime slices, if desired. Serve immediately or refrigerate.

Makes 16 servings

Nutrients per Serving (1 Cake slice):

Calories 136	Protein 4g
Fat <1g	Carbohydrate 30g
Calories from Fat 1%	Fiber <1g
Saturated Fat <1g	Sodium 252mg
Cholesterol 0mg	

Dietary Exchanges: 2 Starch

Luscious Lime Angel Food Cake Roll

Blueberry Bread Pudding with Caramel Sauce

8 slices white bread, cubed
1 cup fresh or frozen blueberries
2 cups skim milk
1 cup EGG BEATERS® Healthy Real Egg Product
²/₃ cup sugar
1 teaspoon vanilla extract
¼ teaspoon ground cinnamon
    Caramel Sauce (recipe follows)

Place bread cubes in bottom of lightly greased 8×8×2-inch baking pan. Sprinkle with blueberries; set aside.

In large bowl, combine milk, Egg Beaters®, sugar, vanilla and cinnamon; pour over bread mixture. Set pan in larger pan filled with 1-inch depth hot water. Bake at 350°F for 1 hour or until knife inserted into center comes out clean. Serve warm with Caramel Sauce.

Makes 9 servings

Caramel Sauce: In small saucepan, over low heat, heat ¼ cup skim milk and 14 vanilla caramels until caramels are melted, stirring frequently.

Prep Time: 20 minutes
Cook Time: 1 hour

Nutrients per Serving (¹/₉ of total recipe):

Calories 196	Protein 7g
Fat 1g	Carbohydrate 40g
Calories from Fat 5%	Fiber 1g
Saturated Fat <1g	Sodium 199mg
Cholesterol 1mg	

Dietary Exchanges: 2 Starch, ½ Fruit, ½ Lean Meat

Blueberry Bread Pudding with Caramel Sauce

Custard Brûlée

>   3 cups fat-free (skim) milk
>   3 eggs
>   4 egg whites
> ½ cup granulated sugar
>   1 teaspoon vanilla
>   1 teaspoon ground cinnamon
>   Ground nutmeg (optional)
> ¼ cup packed light brown sugar

1. Preheat oven to 350°F.

2. Heat milk in 1-quart saucepan over low heat until hot; do not boil.

3. Beat eggs, egg whites and granulated sugar in medium bowl with electric mixer at medium speed 5 minutes or until slightly thickened. Gradually beat in milk and vanilla. Pour milk mixture into 1½-quart soufflé dish or casserole; sprinkle lightly with cinnamon and nutmeg, if desired.

4. Place soufflé dish in roasting pan and place on oven rack; pour 2 inches hot water into roasting pan. Bake, covered, 40 to 50 minutes or until knife inserted halfway between center and edge of custard comes out clean. Cool to room temperature on wire rack. Cover; refrigerate 3 to 4 hours or until chilled.

5. When ready to serve, press brown sugar through a sieve over custard. Broil 4 inches from heat 2 to 3 minutes or until sugar is melted and caramelized. Serve immediately.   **Makes 8 servings**

Nutrients per Serving (⅛ of total recipe):

Calories 146	Protein 7g
Fat 2g	Carbohydrate 24g
Calories from Fat 13%	Fiber 0g
Saturated Fat 1g	Sodium 101mg
Cholesterol 81mg	

Dietary Exchanges: 1½ Starch, ½ Lean Meat

Custard Brûlée

Pumpkin Harvest Bars

1¾ cups all-purpose flour
2 teaspoons baking powder
1 teaspoon grated orange peel
1 teaspoon ground cinnamon
½ teaspoon salt
½ teaspoon ground nutmeg
¼ teaspoon ground ginger
¼ teaspoon ground cloves
¾ cup sugar
½ cup MOTT'S® Natural Apple Sauce
½ cup solid-pack pumpkin
1 whole egg
1 egg white
2 tablespoons vegetable oil
½ cup raisins

1. Preheat oven to 350°F. Spray 13×9-inch baking pan with nonstick cooking spray.

2. In small bowl, combine flour, baking powder, orange peel, cinnamon, salt, nutmeg, ginger and cloves.

3. In large bowl, combine sugar, apple sauce, pumpkin, whole egg, egg white and oil.

4. Add flour mixture to apple sauce mixture; stir until well blended. Stir in raisins. Spread batter into prepared pan.

5. Bake 25 to 30 minutes or until toothpick inserted into center comes out clean. Cool on wire rack 15 minutes; cut into 16 bars.

Makes 16 servings

Nutrients per Serving (1 Bar [¹⁄₁₆ of total recipe]):

Calories 128	Protein 2g
Fat 2g	Carbohydrate 25g
Calories from Fat 15%	Fiber 1g
Saturated Fat <1g	Sodium 143mg
Cholesterol 13mg	

Dietary Exchanges: 1½ Starch, ½ Fat

Pumpkin Harvest Bars

Speedy Pineapple-Lime Sorbet

1 ripe pineapple, cut into cubes (about 4 cups)
⅓ cup frozen limeade concentrate, thawed
1 to 2 tablespoons fresh lime juice
1 teaspoon grated lime peel

1. Arrange pineapple in single layer on large baking pan; freeze at least 1 hour or until very firm. Freeze up to 1 month in resealable plastic freezer food storage bag, if desired.

2. Combine frozen pineapple, limeade concentrate, lime juice and lime peel in food processor; process until smooth and fluffy. If pineapple is not smooth and fluffy, let stand 30 minutes to soften slightly; repeat processing. Garnish as desired. Serve immediately.

Makes 8 servings

Note: This dessert is best if served immediately but may be made ahead, stored in the freezer and softened several minutes before serving.

Nutrients per Serving (½ cup Sorbet [without garnish]):

Calories 56	Protein <1g
Fat <1g	Carbohydrate 15g
Calories from Fat 5%	Fiber 1g
Saturated Fat <1g	Sodium 1mg
Cholesterol 0mg	

Dietary Exchanges: 1 Fruit

Speedy Pineapple-Lime Sorbet

Lemon Raspberry Tiramisu

2 packages (8 ounces each) fat-free cream cheese, softened
6 packets sugar substitute *or* equivalent of ¼ cup sugar
1 teaspoon vanilla
⅓ cup water
1 package (4-serving size) sugar-free lemon-flavored gelatin
2 cups thawed frozen fat-free nondairy whipped topping
½ cup all-fruit red raspberry preserves
¼ cup water
2 tablespoons marsala wine
2 packages (3 ounces each) ladyfingers
1 pint fresh raspberries or frozen unsweetened raspberries, thawed

1. Combine cream cheese, sugar substitute and vanilla in large bowl. Beat at high speed of electric mixer until smooth; set aside.

2. Combine water and gelatin in small microwavable bowl; microwave at HIGH 30 seconds to 1 minute or until water is boiling and gelatin is dissolved. Cool slightly.

3. Add gelatin mixture to cheese mixture; beat 1 minute. Add whipped topping; beat 1 minute more, scraping side of bowl. Set aside.

4. Whisk together preserves, water and marsala in small bowl until well blended. Reserve 2 tablespoons of preserves mixture; set aside. Spread ⅓ cup preserves mixture evenly over bottom of 11×7-inch glass baking dish.

5. Split ladyfingers in half; place half in bottom of baking dish. Spread half of cheese mixture evenly over ladyfingers; sprinkle 1 cup raspberries evenly over cheese mixture. Top with remaining ladyfingers; spread remaining preserves mixture over ladyfingers. Top with remaining cheese mixture. Cover; refrigerate at least 2 hours. Drizzle with reserved 2 tablespoons preserves mixture and sprinkle with remaining raspberries before serving. Garnish as desired. **Makes 12 servings**

continued on page 216

Lemon Raspberry Tiramisu

Lemon Raspberry Tiramisu, continued

Nutrients per Serving (1 slice Tiramisu [$^1/_{12}$ of total recipe] without garnish):

Calories 158	Protein 7g
Fat 1g	Carbohydrate 26g
Calories from Fat 9%	Fiber 1g
Saturated Fat <1g	Sodium 272mg
Cholesterol 52mg	

Dietary Exchanges: 2 Starch

Black Forest Chocolate Fudge Cake

2 cups cake flour
1 cup unsweetened cocoa powder
1 teaspoon baking powder
$^1/_2$ teaspoon salt
1$^1/_2$ cups packed brown sugar
2 eggs
1 egg white
1 cup Dried Plum Purée (recipe follows) or prepared dried plum butter
$^3/_4$ cup nonfat milk
4 teaspoons vanilla
1 cup boiling water
2 tablespoons instant espresso coffee powder
2 teaspoons baking soda
2 cups frozen pitted unsweetened dark sweet cherries, coarsely chopped, thawed and well drained
$^1/_2$ cup chopped toasted walnuts
  Mocha Glaze (recipe follows)
  Chocolate Drizzle (optional, recipe follows)
  Fresh cherries or frozen cherries, thawed
  Mint sprigs for garnish

Preheat oven to 350°F. Coat 12- to 16-cup Bundt or other tube pan with vegetable cooking spray. In large bowl, combine flour, cocoa, baking powder and salt; mix in brown sugar. In medium bowl, whisk eggs, egg white, Dried Plum Purée, milk and vanilla. In 2-cup measure, combine boiling water, espresso powder and baking soda. Stir Dried Plum Purée and water mixtures into flour mixture; mix just until blended. Pour half the batter into prepared pan; sprinkle 2 cups thawed frozen cherries and walnuts evenly over batter. Top with remaining batter. Bake in center of oven about 45 minutes until pick inserted into center comes out clean. Cool in pan on wire rack 15 minutes; remove from pan. Cool completely on wire rack. Prepare Mocha Glaze. Spoon over cake, allowing glaze to run down sides. Prepare Chocolate Drizzle, if desired. Drizzle over glaze. Fill cake center with additional cherries and garnish with mint.

Makes 16 servings

Dried Plum Purée: Combine 1⅓ cups (8 ounces) pitted dried plums and 6 tablespoons hot water in container of food processor or blender. Pulse on and off until dried plums are finely chopped and smooth. Makes 1 cup.

Mocha Glaze: Place 1 cup powdered sugar in small bowl. Dissolve ⅛ teaspoon instant espresso powder in 4 teaspoons water. Stir into sugar until smooth, adding 1 teaspoon water, if needed, for desired consistency.

Chocolate Drizzle: In top of double boiler or bowl set over simmering water, melt 2 tablespoons semisweet chocolate chips. Stir in 2 teaspoons hot water until blended. Cool until desired consistency.

Favorite recipe from **California Dried Plum Board**

Nutrients per Serving (¹⁄₁₆ of cake [with Chocolate Drizzle, but without additional cherries]):

Calories 250	Protein 4g
Fat 3g	Carbohydrate 53g
Calories from Fat 11%	Fiber 2g
Saturated Fat 1g	Sodium 296mg
Cholesterol 27mg	

Dietary Exchanges: 2½ Starch, 1 Fruit, ½ Fat

Acknowledgments

The publisher would like to thank the companies and organizations listed below for the use of their recipes and photographs in this publication.

Birds Eye®

Butterball® Turkey

California Dried Plum Board

Colorado Potato Administrative Committee

ConAgra Foods®

Dole Food Company, Inc.

Egg Beaters®

Equal® sweetener

Guiltless Gourmet®

The Kingsford Products Company

Minnesota Cultivated Wild Rice Council

Mott's® is a registered trademark of Mott's, Inc.

Mrs. Dash®

National Honey Board

National Turkey Federation

New York Apple Association, Inc.

Uncle Ben's Inc.

USA Rice

METRIC CONVERSION CHART

VOLUME MEASUREMENTS (dry)

$^1/_8$ teaspoon = 0.5 mL
$^1/_4$ teaspoon = 1 mL
$^1/_2$ teaspoon = 2 mL
$^3/_4$ teaspoon = 4 mL
1 teaspoon = 5 mL
1 tablespoon = 15 mL
2 tablespoons = 30 mL
$^1/_4$ cup = 60 mL
$^1/_3$ cup = 75 mL
$^1/_2$ cup = 125 mL
$^2/_3$ cup = 150 mL
$^3/_4$ cup = 175 mL
1 cup = 250 mL
2 cups = 1 pint = 500 mL
3 cups = 750 mL
4 cups = 1 quart = 1 L

VOLUME MEASUREMENTS (fluid)

1 fluid ounce (2 tablespoons) = 30 mL
4 fluid ounces ($^1/_2$ cup) = 125 mL
8 fluid ounces (1 cup) = 250 mL
12 fluid ounces (1$^1/_2$ cups) = 375 mL
16 fluid ounces (2 cups) = 500 mL

WEIGHTS (mass)

$^1/_2$ ounce = 15 g
1 ounce = 30 g
3 ounces = 90 g
4 ounces = 120 g
8 ounces = 225 g
10 ounces = 285 g
12 ounces = 360 g
16 ounces = 1 pound = 450 g

DIMENSIONS

$^1/_{16}$ inch = 2 mm
$^1/_8$ inch = 3 mm
$^1/_4$ inch = 6 mm
$^1/_2$ inch = 1.5 cm
$^3/_4$ inch = 2 cm
1 inch = 2.5 cm

OVEN TEMPERATURES

250°F = 120°C
275°F = 140°C
300°F = 150°C
325°F = 160°C
350°F = 180°C
375°F = 190°C
400°F = 200°C
425°F = 220°C
450°F = 230°C

BAKING PAN SIZES

Utensil	Size in Inches/Quarts	Metric Volume	Size in Centimeters
Baking or Cake Pan (square or rectangular)	8×8×2	2 L	20×20×5
	9×9×2	2.5 L	23×23×5
	12×8×2	3 L	30×20×5
	13×9×2	3.5 L	33×23×5
Loaf Pan	8×4×3	1.5 L	20×10×7
	9×5×3	2 L	23×13×7
Round Layer Cake Pan	8×1½	1.2 L	20×4
	9×1½	1.5 L	23×4
Pie Plate	8×1¼	750 mL	20×3
	9×1¼	1 L	23×3
Baking Dish or Casserole	1 quart	1 L	—
	1½ quart	1.5 L	—
	2 quart	2 L	—